"This highly accessible book sheds a developmentally attuned, psychoanalytic perspective on the phenomena of excess in America and shows how it has permeated our culture and collective unconscious. It's wide-ranging critique; from Eve to Lilith, from Hilary Clinton to Angela Markel, and from the baby boomers to generation Z allows the reader to consider the darker aspects of our culture's relationship to excess from a variety of angles, while calling upon the contributions of 21st century Feminist Theory as a path to address the crisis of democracy in America."

Hattie Myers Ph.D. is a training and supervising analyst at (IPTAR) and founder/editor of ROOM: A Sketchbook for Analytic *Action*

"Ireland and Quatman explore the hidden recesses of our national psyche, shedding light on the unconscious forces currently shaping and fragmenting our country. With passion they urge us to embrace a new feminist perspective, one they call "warrior work", to confront the forces that perpetuate sexism, racism and acquisitiveness. This book is a must read, a rallying cry for a society urgently in need of healing."

Kerry Malawista PhD, psychoanalyst, author of *When the Garden isn't Eden and Meet the Moon, and co-chair New Directions Writing Program*

# America's Psychological Now

This book explores the causes behind Trump's victory in the 2016 US presidential election and asks how a psychoanalytic understanding of the social unconscious can help us plot a new direction for the future in US politics and beyond.

It first describes the social/psychological threads that are the now of American culture. Seeds of hope are discovered through an in-depth examination of the American idea of excess as represented by Trump, its archetypal figure. Essential psychoanalytic ideas, such as the fundamental human condition of living with both individual and social unconscious, the psychic feminine principle, the notion of psychic valence and more, are illustrated as psychic integrations necessary for America to move toward a redemptive positive social change. This book combines feminist exploration with playful illustrative imagery and mythic story—aiming to awaken minds across generations.

*America's Psychological Now* is key reading for psychoanalysts, psychologists, political theorists, and anyone wishing to understand better how the social and political systems could be changed for the future.

**Mardy S. Ireland,** PhD, psychologist, psychoanalyst, and educator, retired in October, 2023. She is the author of *The Art of the Subject: Between Necessary Illusion and Speakable Desire in the Analytic Encounter* and *Reconceiving Women: Separating Motherhood from Female Identity,* and a wide range of book chapters and articles.

**Teri Quatman,** PhD, is an Associate Professor of Counseling Psychology in Santa Clara University's Graduate Program of Counseling Psychology and is a psychologist in private practice. She has authored multiple academic publications and two books for clinicians: *Essential Psychodynamic Psychotherapy: An Acquired Art* and *Accessing the Clinical Genius of Winnicott.*

# America's Psychological Now

## Enlivening the Social and Collective Unconscious in a Time of Urgency

Mardy S. Ireland and Teri Quatman

Routledge
Taylor & Francis Group

LONDON AND NEW YORK

Designed cover image: ©Mathew Schwartz

First published 2024
by Routledge
4 Park Square, Milton Park, Abingdon, Oxon OX14 4RN

and by Routledge
605 Third Avenue, New York, NY 10158

*Routledge is an imprint of the Taylor & Francis Group, an informa business*

*British Library Cataloguing-in-Publication Data*
A catalogue record for this book is available from the British Library

ISBN: 9781032677316 (hbk)
ISBN: 9781032677293 (pbk)
ISBN: 9781032677309 (ebk)

DOI: 10.4324/9781032677309

Typeset in Sabon
by Newgen Publishing UK

# Contents

# Illustrations

## Figures

## Tables

# Acknowledgements

Our deep appreciation to the "hands-on" assistance from our illustrator, Silvia Fang, our researcher, Zach Weiss, our art wizard, Tim Lamb, and our draft readers, Susan Orovitz, Kathy Mill, Julie Mitchel, Tedi Uhrowczik, and Suzi Quatman. And also appreciation to our helpful and responsive editors, Kate Hawes and Georgina Clutterbuck, in pulling it all together.

Also, beyond gratitude to the many mentors, colleagues, and patients who have contributed over decades to the making of this book, and to our traveling on this path of psychoanalytic work; with special thanks to those who particularly helped seed this project's developing over time, from the Bay to the Triangle areas: Martine Aniel, Steve Bennet, Sandy Bennet, Chuck Brandes, Heather Craige, Lynn Franco, Alice Jones, Barry Ostrow, Steve Purcell, Patty Rosbrow, Sue Vonbaeyer; and the New Directions Writing Program.

# Permissions

# Part 1

# Threads

# Chapter 1

# In the Beginning

This is an American story, but not solely.

Along with many in America, we believed in 2016 that the time had come for a woman president, and that woman was Hillary Clinton. But the time had *not* come, despite the evidence that the most prepared candidate for president in history lost to a man who was, by far, the least equipped in history. It had been our personal hope that Clinton's election would bring to the presidency a "woman's thinking mind" to bear on the meaning and solutions to America's ills—especially decades of various excesses and expanding inequities.

When Hillary Clinton did not win the election, a fog of trauma enveloped us (and a large swath of America), and numbness made it difficult to find and feel our sadness and despair. Only after finally feeling this sadness for some time could any thinking begin. "Why? What meanings could it hold?" we asked ourselves.

On its face, surely the movement of feminism in the twentieth century had successfully carved an open-enough space for a woman to occupy the presidency. And yet, Clinton did not win. Clear progress for women's rights and freedoms had been made over a century. Arguments and evidence presented over time changed minds and laws as to the rights of women and the places women belonged or could go—that is, primarily, if one were a white, educated woman. Hillary was all those things, and yet, she still did not win.

Where Clinton seemed to offer a "we" way of thinking about issues— "Better Together," Trump promised omnipotence: "I alone can fix it." He combined this with a stark insularity—the concrete insularity of a wall with Mexico, the legal insularity of a ban on Muslims, the economic insularity of destroying free trade agreements with our Pan-Pacific and North American Free Trade partners, and the implied insularity of "white supremacy," foundational to all.

Could it really be possible that in the twenty-first century, people— especially women—could vote for a man who bragged in plain sight, on camera, about his freedom to sexually assault women because when he sees

DOI: 10.4324/9781032677309-2

a beautiful woman, he simply can't help himself? Yes, it was possible—and it happened!

Hillary Clinton has been called (even by herself) a "designated warrior." On the national political stage since her college years, her work as a warrior included much over the decades, but it did not include winning the fight to become president. Given this result, the question arose: Was Hillary Clinton ever truly destined to become the first woman US president? Or was hers another call? Was it her call to do necessary "warrior" work to reveal and combat the forces of sexism—not only conscious sexism, but perhaps more importantly, unconscious sexism.

From the Second World War group work of the psychoanalyst Wilfred Bion, we know that individuals in groups, including within nations, can carry a "valence" or a voice that not only speaks their own ideas, but speaks for a percentage of the group as well.[1] In this respect, Hillary Clinton has done double-duty. She has the valence of carrying the torch of female leadership and empowerment for some in the nation, while simultaneously carrying for others the dark and scary feminine of the witches of Eastwick. Hillary has borne it all—and to a large extent, even in her loss—she has cleared a broader field for the next woman presidential aspirant to compete and win.

A variety of things have been said about why Hillary Clinton lost the 2016 election. For example, that she did not focus enough attention on the suffering of the working class, or that she did not campaign strategically enough in the upper Midwest states. However, there is almost no credible analysis that fails to highlight the impact of sexism upon this historic election—both conscious and unconscious sexism—existing in both genders! It is evident that in fact more "warrior work" is required to break the hold of sexism in our political, economic, and social cultures.

An early twenty-first century global study of women in politics revealed that sexism is the element that best accounts for the low percentage of top female political leaders.[2] Worldwide, women have progressively gained representation in legislatures and parliaments. But reaching the pinnacle of national executive power is indeed another matter. The ubiquity and persistence of sexism appears to be the most powerful explanatory factor across different cultures, even in twenty-first century first-world societies. It seems that there is still something deeply unconscious that may eclipse consciously constructed societal scripts, despite egalitarian leanings and narratives. As of September 2021, of 195 officially recognized countries in the world, only 26 had women as heads of state and/or government. A recent review of gender and world leadership has revealed that in the six decades between 1960 and 2023, there have been only 61 women leaders in world countries (O'Neill, 2023). As of January 2023, only 31 countries have a woman head of state.[3] (The significantly smaller percentage of women CEOs in Fortune 500 business leadership reflects this same trend[4])

So, while various theories have been posited about why Hillary Clinton lost, most pale in comparison to the sheer impact of sexism. Consider, for example, the deep concern over Clinton's use of a private e-mail server versus the ongoing campaign contact between Trump advisors and Russian operatives; and then, of course, Trump's absconding with hundreds of top-secret government files after the 2020 election. Or think about the allegations of financial gain and conflict of interest concerning the Clinton Foundation versus Trump's unwillingness as president to divest from his companies or ever to reveal his tax returns. Or consider the question of who could have made us safer—a candidate with the world experience of a former Secretary of State or the completely inexperienced isolationist Trump? Gender trouble could not have yelled louder!

Something surprising and especially disturbing was also evident in the pattern of female voters in the post-2016 election analyses. The group of women most expected to vote wholeheartedly for Clinton—white, college-educated women—did not! Only 47% voted for Clinton. This is in contrast to 96% of Black women and 59% of Hispanic women who voted for Clinton. And then, after four years of a disheveled and chaotic Trump administration, with a much stronger voter turnout, a *higher* percentage of white women voted for Trump in 2020—55% (Igielnik et al., 2021)!

Embedded and intertwined in this voting pattern is the underlying element of America's enduring, systemic racism. Trump's implicit promise to preserve and bolster white privilege had broad appeal. Not unlike the period of Jim Crow following Reconstruction, Trump's appeal to many in mainstream America signaled a turning backward of any "post-racial" impulse reflected in the election of Barack Obama in 2008 and 2012. Any thought of the Obama presidency as indicative of America's moving forward into a post-racial society was unmasked as the fantasy that it was. Additionally, the intentional recapturing of white privilege was disturbingly reflected in the increase in racially based hate crimes post the 2016 election, and by the explicitly racist policies pursued in Trump's administration (Johnson, 2018).[5]

Initially metabolizing this set of challenges, we (authors) felt a sense of despair that as a nation, and as a species, we have still so far to go. And yet, looking longer and more deliberately, we began to see at least some seeds of hope for the future—a time when women and the notion of what the feminine truly is might come forward to repair and to grace an ailing nation. We found ourselves imagining a new horizon in the "necessary warrior work" of twenty-first century American feminism—specifically, that it's time to move forward from the brand of nineteenth- and twentieth-century feminism that seems to have undervalued the intersectionality of racism and sexism, and their shared unconscious roots. It's now much clearer that the twenty-first century feminist color of change must be polychromatic!

## The Geode

Trump's sexism and racism were, and are, parts of the multiple human excesses his language reflects. He is nothing if not excess! In fact, the word "excess" itself became like a geode in our minds—looking simple and rough on the outside, but having a more intricate pattern within. As with any geode, the concept of excess and the word itself have required a certain force to break open. In so doing, we found this word to be multi-dimensional, paradoxical, and freighted with directional signage—all needing to be examined.[6]

How did this man who rode down a gilded escalator to his entrance into the race, who decried Mexicans as rapists and Muslims as anti-American, who flaunted his personal wealth at every turn, who valued women primarily for their sexual appeal to him, who bent the rules of office to the breaking point of two impeachments—how did this mere man rise to the pinnacle of power in the most powerful nation on earth? What about his *excesses* stirred the imaginations of the dispossessed among the citizenry as well as the rank-and-file? What about his politics of grievance inspired followership to the point of violence on January 6, 2021, and presaged even more violence following the FBI search for classified documents at Mar-a-Lago? We wanted to look specifically at this geode of excess in America and its link to the response to Trump. We follow this theme in Chapter 3.

## A Tipping Point

The choice of Trump over Clinton was really nothing new. Men win. Yet this particular win was a dramatic display of something hidden beneath this long-accepted pattern. For some, Trump represents the last desperate hope for saving and preserving white American privilege and exceptionalism. Yet at the same time, Trump's presidency was a four-year demonstration of what failing to pay attention to unconscious elements in the culture (sexism, racism, misogyny, xenophobia, avarice) looks and feels like. Given these elements, we must wonder if what he has really represented is the last desperate gasp of patriarchy. Further, we are asking if the Trump presidency—followed by "Trumpism"—is reflecting a final acute unconscious eruption of America's own excesses that is demanding attention and accountability.

As psychoanalytic clinicians, we are aware of how very much the unconscious features significantly in human functioning—not only individually, but at the group and societal level as well. We know from clinical practice and research that when something has, over a long time, been denied, repressed, or projected onto others, there can be an eruption from the unconscious within. This eruption can be more violent—demanding more attention, and often, can be more destructive in its consequences—than if the earlier clues and psychic messages had been decoded earlier. Today America's democracy is deeply threatened by just such an eruption. It follows upon the long-term denial of multiple unconscious elements—elements that have seeded the current political polarization in which both racism and sexism are deeply embedded.

Decades of accumulating forms of excess—for example, increasing economic inequities, ongoing racist police killings, spiraling opiate addiction, increasing mass shootings, increasing homelessness—plus the unfolding of "Trumpism" ripples during and after the 2020 election—may only be some of the signs of America's approaching a psychological tipping point.

Trump denied the reality of his 2020 defeat while continuing to hold a long, extended campaign to recapture the presidency. Shortly after a dismal show of his endorsed candidates in the 2022 mid-term elections, he announced this third campaign for the US presidency. His campaign has been indulged and exploited by the acolytes within his own party—effectively gathering a gang around him of "wannabe bullies," sycophants, pragmatic strategists, and others who were simply afraid of retaliation should they challenge him. But what if this excessive <u>grasp</u> is really a last <u>gasp</u>? What if Trump and "Trumpism" place us on the precipice of an entirely different model of executive leadership for the twenty-first century?

In the context of this possible tipping point, we see twenty-first century feminism as potentially midwifing the birth of a transformational idea—an idea a long time in coming.[7] This "slow idea" concerns how much the unconscious is a significant player in human functioning—certainly in individuals—but also in nations/groups as well.[8] It may be time for citizens of America to recognize (and integrate) the unconscious aspects of our culture—as foundational to our notions of social justice and ethical behavior. The election of 2020 and the proximity of the 2024 elections have impelled us (as citizens, but also as psychologists) into the project of understanding, at a deeper level, this phase of the "warrior work" that indeed twenty-first century feminism may champion.

## In Closing—The Opening

For these two white women of privilege—both clinicians, of the baby boomer generation—the 2016 and 2020 elections magnified the irrepressible and painful conundrum of gender, race, and political power in the USA. In the emotionally charged intersection of unconscious sexism and racism (54% of white women in 2016 and 55% in 2020 voted for Trump), combined with America's extended relationship to excess, we ourselves heard a "call to arms." This book has been a response to that call.[9]

It is our belief that twenty-first century feminism can be a leading force in the necessary "warrior work" ahead—that of bringing the collective/social unconscious more to life in our American culture. Such a movement has the potential to bring about a powerful transformation in how the culture understands both our shared humanity and our shared history. As Martin Luther

King noted, "The arc of the moral universe is long, but it bends toward justice." It may also be—and this is our hope—that such a transformative understanding of the role of unconscious elements in America's history and its troubled present might bring a hastening of true social justice and further human understanding.

The "call to arms" as we have heard it is to hold, to carry, and to defend two interwoven ideas of this century: (1) the inviolate dignity of, and justice for, each and every human being regardless of gender, race, or any other claimed identity; and (2) the necessity for an absolute and ongoing recognition of the unconscious elements of the human mind within groups and nations, for better and for worse, that <u>must</u> be factored into conscious social/ governmental policy-making as a means to help safeguard human equality and dignity.[10] Achieving these goals would represent an "American exceptionalism" worth celebrating, and worth exporting, exercising America's world leadership to encourage others to do the same. America clearly has a complex story of unconscious elements to own and examine, but this task is certainly not solely (or soul-y) an American story, but an awaiting global project as well.

In the next chapters, we will develop the threads of twenty-first century warrior work—presenting this weaving as both aspirational and inspirational—combining both our thoughts and musings of serious intent with a playfulness in imagery and story, in an effort to reach younger generations as well.

In Chapter 2 we begin this weaving through words and also a figure drawing of the multi-dimensional notion of the unconscious mind—so necessary to any imagining as to how we might re-knit a fractured and fractious American culture, a culture still in deep struggle with the castes of gender and race, personified in whom we choose to represent us in this struggle.

## Notes

1  See Wilfred Bion (1989). In a similar manner, Obama carried the valence and voice of America's hope of a non-racist future that is not yet realized—nor can it be—without a national working-through process concerning its dark foundation of slavery and subsequent systemic racism.

2  See Corbett et al. (2022).

3  This according to the UN Women report: *Facts and figures: Women's leadership and political participation* (2023, March 7); and underlining that gender parity in the realm of politics remains yet to be realized.

4  This according to US Bureau of Labor Statistics 2023—there were 44 female chief executives spearheading America's Fortune 500 companies, with women leading only 8.8% of businesses on the 2022 list.

5  Hate crimes also increased by 20% in 2021 as hateful rhetoric also increased post-January 6 insurrection. Also, *The Year in Hate & Extremism Report 2021* (2022, March 3), Southern Poverty Law Center.

6  Again, the analyst Wilfred Bion (1962) noted that in an analyst, frequent experiences build over time to an accumulated "saturation" point within the analyst,

wherein the analyst then becomes able to put together thoughts and words in an interpretation that moves the work forward. This reflected the process the authors experienced precipitating the word and geode of excess.

7 Atul Gawande (July 22, 2013) coined the term "slow idea" during his exploration of the role of bacteria in human healing, where more than two centuries were needed to make the link between bacteria and illness. History is replete with examples of ideas whose roots germinate for decades, even centuries, before their bloom comes forth into broad acceptance.

8 Is the bulging mental health crisis wherein there are simply not enough clinicians to meet the current national needs yet another indication that it is time for a cultural shift concerning mental health? One where the small sub-set of psychoanalysts and therapists who attend specifically to unconscious elements in a people's sufferings no longer remain the sole shepherds of the unconscious of the nation? To pursue this idea, see Bion, *Experiences in Groups, and Other Papers.*

9 This was another part of that process where Wilford Bion talks about how in an analysis, the analyst can be overwhelmed and confused and at times needs to sit with these feelings until they reach a certain "saturation" point, at which time words to say precipitate out of those saturated, formerly unspeakable, experiences.

10 In this respect our effort here is one of moving the "psychoanalytic sensibility" from the clinical office to society at large—something the French analyst Lacan referred to as "psychoanalysis in extension."

## References

Bion, W. R. (1962). *Learning From Experience.* Karnac.

Bion, W. R. (1969). *Experiences in Groups, and Other Papers.* Tavistock/Routledge.

Corbett, C., et al. (2022). Pragmatic bias impedes women's access to political leadership, *Proceedings of the National Academy of Sciences, 119*: 6, February 1, e2112616119. https://doi.org/10.1073/pnas.2112616119

Gawande, A. (2013). Sharing slow ideas. *The New Yorker*, July 22. https://www.newyorker.com/magazine/2013/07/29/slow-ideas

Igielnik, R., Keeter, S., & Hartig, H. (2021). Behind Biden's 2020 victory: An examination of the 2020 electorate, based on validated voters. Pew Research Center, June 30. https://www.pewresearch.org/politics/2021/06/30/behind-bidens-2020-victory/.

Johnson, D. (2018). Report: Rise in hate violence tied to 2016 presidential election. Southern Poverty Law Center, March 1. https://www.splcenter.org/hatewatch/2018/03/01/report-rise-hate-violence-tied-2016-presidential-election

O'Neill, A. (2023). Number of countries where the de facto highest position of executive power was held by a woman from 1960 to 2023. Statista, January 2. https://www.statista.com/statistics/1058345/countries-with-women-highest-position-executive-power-since-1960/

*The Year in Hate & Extremism Report 2021* (2022). Southern Poverty Law Center, March 3. https://www.splcenter.org/20220309/year-hate-extremism-report-2021

UN Women. Facts and figures: Women's leadership and political participation (2023). March 7. https://www.unwomen.org/en/what-we-do/leadership-and-political-participation/facts-and-figures#_ednref2

US Bureau of Labor Statistics (2023). Employed persons by detailed occupation, sex, race, and Hispanic or Latino ethnicity, January 25. https://www.bls.gov/cps/cpsaat11.htm#:~:text=1%2C669-

US Department of Justice, FBI, Criminal Justice Information Services Division (2023). March, Supplemental Hate Crime Statistics, 2021. https://cde.ucr.cjis.gov/LATEST/webapp/#/pages/explorer/crime/hate-crime

World Economic Forum (2022). *Global Gender Gap Report 2022*. https://www3.weforum.org/docs/WEF_GGGR_2022.pdf

# Chapter 2

# Living in Denial

## Our Multi-Dimensional Unconscious

To begin our weaving, a brief exploration of the concept of "the unconscious" as a central strand of our story is necessary for what will follow.[1]

The word "unconscious" includes an array of phenomena but refers broadly to things that exist outside our conscious mind at any given moment. It can be thought of as both a place within us and a process within us that can motivate us beyond our conscious knowings.[2] Patterns, attractions, attitudes, impulses, loves, hates, stuck-points are all examples of things that move us without our explicit conscious direction.

Figure 2.1 shows a simplified drawing to illustrate aspects of the different areas within this territory—"the unconscious."

Imagine a cross-sectional image of a person standing on a small island. In this drawing, we can see under the surface three depth levels of the sea— the shallowest waves, the mid-level depths, and the deepest level up from the ocean floor itself. As is evident, the person and the island itself are not really detached from the ocean bottom—it just looks like it because the island appears on top of the water. And while this water is named as different oceans, seas, bays across geographical locations, the reality is that, mostly, the water flows throughout the planet and connects all parts of our human globe. Metaphorically, this speaks to the shared human condition of unconscious waters below our individual conscious identities.

### Level 1 of The Unconscious—The Ocean Depths

At the deepest level, farthest from the surface, it is darker and murkier—and it's harder to see what might be there, moving about in this water. Also, now add to this picture a sound track accompanying these currents and moving elements—a voice and musical track that will change somewhat at each ascending depth level. This sound track is laid down in our early infant history, and is unique to each one of us, but it will also share some sound and emotional and thematic elements derived from the language and culture that precedes us and into which we were born.[3]

DOI: 10.4324/9781032677309-3

*Figure 2.1* The Unconscious
Artist to be credited in acknowledgements

This level of the sea starting at the ocean floor corresponds to the deepest part of the unconscious in our minds, or our "psyches." It is formed in us as babies, coming into being before we have of a real sense of any individual self-ness or any language with which to make sense of our experiences. The process of how we are cared for by parents or primary others installs certain emotional fundamentals within us. Is life safe or unsafe? Do my cries elicit love or resentment? Additionally, those responses to us are invariably influenced by the cultural context (that is, how babies are to be cared for and children raised, etc.) within which both caretaker and baby live.

Our earliest times set the parameters for how we will take in and make sense of others and ourselves in the future. This time (before the age of around two years) is a world full of bits of sensations, emotions and sounds, bits of meanings not yet understood, in which we are submerged. In fact, at first, we only experience language as emotionally-felt sounds coming from mother and primary others that land on our ears and our bodies as pleasurable or not. These are all building elements of our human psyches. We don't remember this time, but it is nonetheless formative of who we will later become.

At this level, we are closest to being instinctual animals, but we are already on our way to becoming a hybrid creature—instinctual at root, but soon to have our sense of self organized via certain images and (later) words and language.

The developmental achievements of these early months and first years will become the realm of what has been termed by neurobiologists as "implicit memory"—emotions, behaviors, sensations that just *are* inside us and are a part of our unconscious minds. We do not have to think about these things, and don't experience them as memories—we just *feel* them, we just *know* them, we just *do* them.[4]

This level of the unconscious informs our felt self. Do we feel secure and safe? Do we feel received? Do we feel insignificant? Are we recognized in a way we can feel? Do we feel embodied? Do we feel embattled? Can we expect goodness? This level of the unconscious may govern some of what shrewd political candidates appeal to (for example, that George W. Bush was the candidate people felt they could "have a beer with").

## Level 2—The Dynamic Unconscious

Moving upward in our drawing of unconscious territory, to the next water level, things become more visible. We can now see recognizable images of many kinds—compelling, confusing, scary, positive and negative, things moving about in the water accompanied perhaps by a more complex sound-track. So, as we develop, we gradually become speaking, remembering, and fantasy-making creatures. And once we fully become speaking creatures, the time before is left behind—unremembered in our conscious minds. So, our acquisition of language, while developmentally powerful, creates a human paradox: it makes us profoundly divided creatures. There is what is instinctual and what is not; what is conscious and what is not; what is remembered and what is not; what can be expressed in language and what cannot.

We all live within this paradox. Language actually carves a space of missing-ness in us, psychically; because while there is always a part of our experience that language can scoop up and express, there is also always some part—sometimes the most important part—that is beyond the power of language to contain or express. (For example, what does it mean to say, "I love you" or, "My child has died"?) In other words, there lives something in us that is beyond language. And, it will have its say—somewhere, somehow, sometime in our daily lives.

So, Level 2 of the ocean, often called the "dynamic unconscious," is a region that includes experiences in memories, fantasies, and thoughts that we may have partial access to, but are not in our conscious minds at the moment. This level of the unconscious is bi-directional: it contains things that can flow up from our deepest unconscious depths, and things that we push down from our consciousness into our unconscious.

Things that flow upward from our unconscious depths might include elements of our instinctual animal selves seeking more expression and greater form. Or it might include what you used to experience as a pre-verbal child, bodily and emotionally, when mom and dad were violent with each other. Or it might be a set of sad and angry thoughts tied to a past loss, and which have been kept away from consciousness, but can push upward in certain circumstances that are triggering to us.

Things that we push downward can include things that we simply don't want to think about or feel (for example, we try to push traumatic scenes away from our consciousness). Feelings, thoughts, and impulses in ourselves that feel unacceptable can also be banned from the conscious region of our minds and pushed back into this unconscious space/realm. Such banishment, however, is not once and for all. This banishment, referred to as "repression," is an ongoing process, requiring our psychic energy to keep those things out of our conscious minds.[5]

Sometimes there may be elements below the level of the conscious mind (that may have been pushed into the unconscious) which strongly seek a return to consciousness—exerting a forceful push for recognition as a way for our psyche to reach for more psychic integration. This psychic activity is called the "return of the repressed," and it will come into play in several subsequent chapters, starting with Chapter 7.[6]

Thus, the "dynamic unconscious" is a lively, ongoing place and process within all our everyday human experience—as much as anything is—regarding who we think we are in our day-to-day lives, and regarding how we imagine and construe what others are "up to," so to speak. This is the place of our dreams as well.

### Living within Intersections

These two regions (Levels 1 and 2) are perhaps the most significant parts of the "unconscious mind." Yet, there is a third region of the unconscious territory (Level 3), seen in Figure 2.1 as those very shallow waves lapping at the person's feet. A name for this region is the "pre-conscious mind." These are things just barely out of one's conscious mind, but which are relatively easy to reach and bring back into mind.

In the two deepest parts of the unconscious mind (Level 1 and Level 2), elements can also get "assigned to" or projected onto other people—in both positive and negative ways—as traits or beliefs about the other, but that are, in actuality, aspects of ourselves. This psychic process is called "projection." (Perhaps you may have seen this process exhibited in yourself, others you know, or, with some frequency, by our former president.) Such an unconscious process, in a sense, can determine many of our conscious intentions and scripts—much more than most of us think it to be so. (Projection is another unconscious process salient to the next chapter and beyond.)

Were the unconscious just an empty space, it would be of no consequence. Oddly, this is how most individuals in our culture actually think about it—or, more correctly, don't think about it at all! The first few years of childhood live inside us with significant unconscious effects on our lives. But, in fact, we live with this permeable membrane between unconscious and conscious parts of the mind—making it unclear who's on first some of the time, or who is pitching in any particular inning in our game of life! It is simply easier, but not accurate, for everyone to pretend that only the conscious mind matters—and that matters of the unconscious mind don't.

No one can empty out the unconscious into consciousness and thereby make everything whole in their conscious self. It is simply the human condition that we are bicameral creatures, where aspects of both regions of our minds participate at every level in our day-to-day life, and color our experiences. This is true whether we engage intentionally with this reality or not.

Recognizing, however, and having an appreciation of—having a workable relationship with—the flow between the unconscious and conscious parts of one's mind makes a crucial difference in terms of becoming one's fullest and most aware self in that unfolding process of one's particular life. Socrates' reflection that "… an unexamined life is not worth living" was very likely pointing to this fact. When someone enters psychological treatment, they often want something to be "fixed." But often their suffering is attached in part to a past "something" that in itself cannot be undone. Most clinicians focus on symptom-relief directly—dealing with things purely, or primarily, on a conscious level. This may be sufficient for some, or even desired. But it will not be sufficient or solely desired by others. Some clinicians committed to working in the intersectional territory between unconscious and conscious minds will more likely be aware that they cannot fix or undo the past as such, but can help reshape how a person experiences their current situation/suffering and their psychological stance in their life more generally, and thus will come to experience their past, their present, and their future quite differently in the course of their therapeutic work.[7]

## The Social Group and The Collective Unconscious

And finally, *here is the thing*: not only every person, but also every culture/ nation has unconscious elements that swim beneath the surface of its collective, conscious identity, and that nonetheless affect and move its people as a group.[8] Within any culture/nation, there are also embedded smaller subgroups carrying additional influential unconscious elements.[9] Yes, it is a lot to deal with!

For example, culturally, we might point to a shared emotional heritage as the forerunner adventurers, looking to establish a new life in America with new freedoms. We might point to a shared emotional heritage as waves of Americans experienced being initially shunned as immigrants, or as the descendants of subsequent waves of immigrants seeking the promise of a new land, as parts of our collective unconscious. We also unconsciously carry the affective remnants of being a nation founded in political protest, and one built on the labor of enslaved Africans.[10] We bear the unconscious emotional stain of having appropriated lands and decimated indigenous peoples. We also might point to our progressive, unrelenting forward creative push toward the edges of the frontier, geographically and emotionally, imagined as part of both our conscious and unconscious collective minds. We might even see the notion of American exceptionalism as an elemental current within our collective mind. These collective parts are foundational, and they form the ever-moving unconscious currents of who we are as an American culture. And just as an individual person is at times psychically subjected to the press of a "return of the repressed" in themselves, so too does this occur within established groups and nations.[11] This is the territory we explore in the realm of America's decades of excess—especially in the work of gender and racial equality.

Thus, springing from the idea that there are indeed collective or social unconscious ideational and emotional currents, intermixed with the individual's ocean depths of the unconscious, we now move onward to Chapter 3 to look into the multifaceted phenomenon of excess, its varied manifestations, and multiple meanings in American society as it culminated and expressed itself in the pinnacle figure of Donald Trump, and the toxic spill into "Trumpism."

## Notes

1  In the vein of both (Hillary) Clinton and Trump being individuals who psychically carry certain elements/themes for the nation/group, a relatively small group of psychoanalysts, psychoanalytic psychotherapists, writers, and theorists have also carried the unconscious aspects of mind, not only for self-selecting individuals seeking treatment, as well as themselves, but also, for the nation at large. Thus the weaving that begins with this thread hopefully promotes greater awareness within a larger group of citizens concerning the power and reach of unconscious influences in their lives and in the in nation in which we live.

2  Freud (1912) brought the unconscious into greater public view through his development of the clinical treatment of psychoanalysis. He described it differently across time. LaPlanche and Pontalis (1973) offer a good and brief summary of this evolving concept. Jacques Lacan brought language into play at the different levels of the unconscious as noted in Figure 2.1—but it is not an accurate interpretation, sometimes ascribed to Lacan, that his words "the unconscious is structured like a language" ever meant the unconscious is only composed of language. Also, the concept of "dissociation" and its relationship to the concept of "repression" is beyond the scope of this presentation. It is complex and complicated territory, that traumatic experiences wrought by war, catastrophic societal events, sexual, physical, and emotional abuse have required additional ways of thinking. Terms like fluid and fluctuating self-states, splitting of the ego, and traumatic kernels/states all refer to more, or less, encapsulated states of mind. This is to say that, in the extreme, we see a loss of linkage among our fluid self-states and to our own central organized and organizing self, resulting in multiple personality

disorders, a loss of one's sense of self, or even a repeated sense of falling into a prior trauma experience (or as a defense against anticipated trauma).

Where there is a vertical division between conscious and unconscious, dissociative states are horizontal splits/divisions. A trigger, consciously experienced, will throw the individual into another painful state of mind that includes both conscious and unconscious elements—i.e., primitive emotions of terror, images and fragments thereof, or sounds, as in pieces of words and/or just voices. Imagine if, in the illustration in Figure 2.1, there were string coming from the figure's head attached to a big helium balloon, or various smaller sized balloons; a balloon filled with scary bits of experience or nothingness itself that live separately from the figure's regular thinking-feeling self; where along the slip line of that string, they could slip into a separate reality in certain moment; you are getting the idea of it.

In the realm of neuroscience there is an entirely different vocabulary for describing "implicit" versus "explicit" feeling, thinking, and behavior. For example, Decety and Cacioppo (2011).

3  The power of sound as music in, and surrounding, language elements that precedes its meanings begins us. And it is said that sound is the last sensory dimension we lose in our process of dying. The Lacanian analyst, Serge LeClaire, has said at this deepest level of the unconscious that if someone could say/sing the particular series of letters unique to that person's history, you could induce in them a state of ecstasy—be that euphoria or excruciating pain, or both!>

4  See Daniel Siegal's very accessible (2012) book.

5  See Freud's writings on *The Unconscious* (1912), *Interpretation of Dreams* (1900) and *Repression* (1915) in *The Standard Edition of the Complete Psychological Works of Sigmund Freud*.

6  For a more, albeit brief, description on "return of the repressed", see LaPlanche and Pontalis (1973).

7  This is a shorthand explanation of the difference between a psychoanalyst or psychoanalytically oriented psychotherapist and that of many other kinds of trained mental health workers and psychotherapists—be they psychologists, social workers, psychiatrists, or counselors.

8  Carl Jung (1936) was the analyst to bring the notion of a "collective unconscious" into consideration and development in psychoanalysis beyond Freud's notion of inherited patterns. It was a place of theoretical conflict and elemental to their going their separate ways in the evolution of psychoanalysis. Jung thought the collective unconscious was structural to the notion of the unconscious. Here, we are focusing on the unconscious aspect of organized groups—including nations/societies—that reflect a particular socio-cultural context and history.

9  The ever-insolvable human puzzle: Does identity begin externally, as brought to us by others, or internally, that we extend to become ourselves and others reflect or mirror this back to us? Or perhaps some schema involving both, as in M. C. Escher's hands, drawing each other?

10 Making things even more layered, particular sub-groups within larger groups can have both shared and differing social unconscious elements. For example, racial identity in America carries both. Layton (2020) speaks to our own sub-group of white psychoanalysts focuses on normative unconscious processes within privileged whites. In contrast, the work of Stoute and Slevin (2023) speaks to the unconscious affective defense of rage in Black people as a necessary element for

survival, and to even thrive, after the trauma of enslavement in America and the continued persecution and disenfranchisement that has followed.

11  Within sub-groups we can also see the "return of the repressed." Carl Jung and the American analyst, Trigant Burrow, who brought forward notions of collective or social unconscious, were both expunged from psychoanalysis. Dijani (2022) has nicely summarized signs in the last decades of a return of this theme of group unconscious—proposing an umbrella term of "social unconscious."

## References

Burrow, T. (1927). *The Social Basis of Consciousness*. Andesite Press.

Decety, J., & Cacioppo, J. (eds) (2011). *The Oxford Handbook of Social Neuroscience*. Oxford University Press. See also Baars, B., & Cage, N. (2010) (2e). *Cognition, Brain and Consciousness: Introduction to Cognitive Neuroscience*. Academic Press.

Dijani, K. G. (2022). The social unconscious: Then and now. *International Journal of Applied Psychoanalytic Studies, 19*, 179–186.

Freud, S. (1912). A note on the unconscious in psycho-analysis. *The Standard Edition of the Complete Psychological Works of Sigmund Freud, 12*, 255–266. Also in Standard Edition, *Interpretation of Dreams* (1900) and *Repression* (1915).

Jung, C. (1936). *The Concept of the Collective Unconscious*. Collected Works, 9, 1. Princeton University Press.

LaPlanche, J., & Pontalis, J. (1973). *The Language of Psychoanalysis*. W. W. Norton & Company.

Layton, L. (2020). *Toward a Social Psychoanalysis: Culture, Character, and Normative Unconscious Processes*. Routledge.

LeClaire, S. (1998). *Psychoanalyzing: On the Order of the Unconscious and the Practice of the Letter*. Stanford University Press.

Siegel, D. J. (2012) (2e). *The Developing Mind: How Relationships and the Brain Interact to Shape Who We Are*. Guilford Press.

Stoute, B., & Slevin, M. (eds) (2023). Black Rage: The psychic adaption to the trauma of oppression, Chapter 10 in *The Trauma of Racism: Lessons From the Therapeutic Encounter*. Routledge.

# Chapter 3

# Cracking the Geode of Excess

Turning on the television, the cries of "Trump! Trump! Trump!" resounds at a rally in my hometown of Raleigh, NC. (His family's original name, "Drumpf," would not have been so catchy!) I feel my fellow Carolinians' emotional calling. But as a psychoanalyst, I also reflect on the thought that my fellow citizen Americans were playing a "trump card" in the 2016 election. And what does a trump card do? It is a card that plays at a higher value than its actual value in the game at hand.

Indeed, the playing of that trump card did shift the political game in 2016 in North Carolina and beyond! In the 2016 election, North Carolina turned from blue to red. North Carolina sat then, as it did again in the 2020 election, and now as the 2024 election approaches, squarely at the table of a very new political game: Democracy itself is on the table. Trump's ultimate game is one wherein the function of words and the meanings behind them become unfettered to the truths they were meant to represent. Is something true because it is stated by a prominent leader, or is it true because its veracity rests on a foundation apart from its mouthpiece? Language exists, at least in part, to set limits on conniving distortions. But language itself was repeatedly attacked in 2016 and even more so thereafter, with increasingly damaging results for democracy and society itself.

Looking back, from early in the 2016 election campaign and then reprised in the 2020 election, there was a word that was not spoken extensively but did push its way onto the political scene. Its very absence was an assault on the truth! That word was "excess." It took its unconscious place, becoming louder and more insistent, at first affixed only to Donald Trump, as he rode the "Trump Tower" escalator down to the staging area below, flaunting his extravagant wealth, and talking his outsized policy ideas (for example, mass deportation of 11 million "illegals"). But oddly, the word "excess" also became velcroed to Hillary Clinton. The idea of her "privilege" to act "outside the rules" with her female "entitlement" to the presidency itself, and her private e-mail server looming in the background, all caused a wave of uncertainty about her motivations and character.

DOI: 10.4324/9781032677309-4

The excess associated with both candidates provoked more than the usual questions of "What is behind this?" as in "What are these candidates really saying?" or "What motivates their pursuit of the presidency?" In so many ways, there was the emanation of questions underneath it all, such as, "What is 'unconsciously' motivating their conscious talk?" And perhaps because of this, more than any presidential contest in our boomer lifetimes, journalists' comments such as, "I am not a psychiatrist or psychologist but ..." or "We need a psychoanalyst to ..." were strewn across the 2016 election coverage. In other words, we were all left wondering what was beyond both Trump's and Clinton's "excesses" and their consciously worded intentions about becoming president.

Thus it was that the collective unconscious insistently pulled the word "excess" into our view, or at least into our consciousness, during the 2016 election and in the administration that followed. "Excess" and its links to the unconscious held its place in our minds ever more firmly as we lived through the years of words and actions of the Trump administration, with Trump playing his "trump card" again and again within the hallowed framework of our democratic institutions. Perhaps even more disturbing (if that were possible) was his evolution into "Bully in Chief," as he has continued to insinuate himself into the workings of, and continued influence upon, the Republican party after his 2020 loss.

There was much to understand about the decades of accumulated excess that we simply did not yet comprehend in 2016. Why would Donald Trump, Mr Excess *par excellence*, be elected in 2016? What is it that we did not "get" about America's state of "not well-being" from our decades-long experience of excesses, such that we needed four intense years of excess to function as a psychological flashpoint of distress? And what are we to make of the accentuation of Trump's excesses in "Trumpism's" arising? How do we make sense of the fact that even though Biden/Harris won the election by over 7 million votes, Trump, nonetheless, received approximately 73 million votes, and more votes from both white women and at least one racial minority group in 2020 than in 2016? How do we make sense of the millions of American voters who are now willing, in a potential second Trump presidency, to follow Trump's lead into a new America—one led by an autocrat-in-waiting who is already making plans to radically concentrate power in his presidency in himself. As we write this book, he is actively forging plans to "dismantle" the administrative state, bringing such agencies as the Department of Justice (DoJ), FBI, and the Internal Revenue Service under his direct control. (The DoJ could then be used to pursue his political enemies.) If he were unchecked in his power, we could also anticipate that he would change other structures of government and perhaps even alter the constitution itself. Why not? So, what do we make of the millions of voters seemingly willing follow such a figure, such an omnipotent, aggressive "other" who promises to right the economic and social ills they have suffered in current-day America? How do we make sense of it?

We made of it the following. That Donald Trump is a kind of icon of excess, and that excess speaks to the deeper and darker aspects of America's collective/social unconscious. When the body spikes a fever, it signals that there is an underlying problem. Likewise, when the psyche has a fever, we see intra- and inter-personal dysfunction at the surface. When a culture spikes a fever—when it devolves, in essence—it also sends a message. What is that message? It is certainly multifaceted, but at least in part it may relate to undeciphered messages of our culture's unconscious relationship to its own excesses.

And, if this is the case, then we see Trump as personifying—and yes, even celebrating—all the varied aspects of excess. We see in him the representation of the dark side of capitalism—the side that is solipsistic—that cares for nothing beyond its own wealth, its own prominence, its own glorification. We also see in him a representation of the last desperate gasp of misogyny, xenophobia, and patriarchy in American culture, straining to recapture its hold on a culture clearly in transition. It may be the last gasp of an element that is desiccating—but a gasp which has nonetheless accrued power and momentum toward subverting American democratic principles and structures!

In saying both these things, the suggestion here is that Trump is a "parallactic" figure. Parallax refers to seeing an object as somehow different simply as a result of looking at that object from different positions. With Donald Trump, it is impossible to be on a straight line viewing him—or to even get a straight word out of him! He has been differentially described as a messiah or dangerous destroyer, depending upon one's vantage point. But, if there is any one thing that bridges this difference in viewing angles, it is the Excess, and the multifaceted meanings of Excess, beyond even Trump himself, that has insistently called for attention, explication, and examination.

Why did Excess so capture our attention in 2016 and seems still to do so in the phenomenon of "Trumpism"? Why did we tolerate it, and—for a third of the country—celebrate it in Trump? What does it tell us about ourselves and about the culture we have built?

## Language as a Living Thing

In pursuing this question of Trumpian excess, it is important to remind ourselves that language is truly a living thing. Some words come alive in popular parlance, stay for a while, and disappear—much like an object bobbing in a river's current, only to go under water, and rarely to be seen again (for example, the word "knave"). Other words have an enduring, consistent meaning across time, space and cultures. Still other words accumulate new elements to their meaning across time, like stringing new beads onto a necklace. Such is the case with the word "excess." Words like excess have staying power; they force themselves into our ways of talking and thinking over time—and they become more complex in their meanings through time, reflecting the complicated nature of human development.

So, come along with us as we examine this word "excess"—so important in our effort to understand where we are in American culture today—tracing it from its first Western recorded etymological beginnings to help us understand where we find ourselves now, and how we can think about going forward from here.

## The Multiple Meanings of Excess

The word "excess" was first recorded in Western civilization within the multiple lexicons of Middle English, Anglo-French, and Late Latin languages in the late fourteenth century. The original fourteenth-century Old French definition of excess stressed "extravagance or outrage," framing excess in terms of morality and judgment.[1]

Trump is immediately recognizable in this most commonly used definition of excess. In this, we see excess as greed, unmasked; greed disguised as "fortune," but more like a peacock flaunting his feathers. And yet, there is much more to the making of Trump as a capstone of America's years of excess. This first definition, however, does remain close to how we most often use the word "excess" in everyday conversation. And while we all do have an intuitive sense for the good or ordinary kind of excess, we also do know outrageous excess when we see it. Excess as in all the billionaire Wall Street bankers whom ordinary Americans bailed out of bankruptcy during the 2008 recession, or in President Trump's multiple golf trips to his own private courses (281 visits, to be exact), of which the first four alone cost American tax payers over 13 million dollars in 2017, according to a GAO report.[2] The point of this excess is inequality: to establish the "haves" as higher on the "great chain of being" than the "have nots."

Because of the unbridled and repetitive excesses of the Trump years, a hidden element of this kind of excess has been laid bare. Specifically, this extreme of excess depends in large part for its existence upon an over-embracing of the masculine at the expense of the feminine. The masculine, in Jungian psychology, refers to a set of characteristics that, in their mature form, include task-orientation, self-mastery, assertiveness, directness and honest forthrightness, but in their immature form include self-absorption, ego-motivation, self-pity, selfishness, defensiveness, aggression, rationalization, and regression under stress.[3] The positive feminine, in contrast, refers in part to the quality of intentional, related attunement devoted to both the being and the development of an other—and also a capacity to move with the flow of things while also attuning to the inner world and embracing creativity and play.[4] We are all meant to have both aspects within us. But we see clearly in Trump's brand of extravagant excess the absence of relational empathy to guide both sentiment and ethic—an absence of the positive feminine.

Historically, it has been women who devote themselves to the first years of the work of bringing a civilized human being into a family and then into a society. The early experience of being attended to in our development is something none of us really remembers or can talk about since it goes on before we even become remembering little creatures. This explains how this crucial task of the feminine can, in many cultures, be designated as "unimportant" work. Truly, it is often only noticed in its absence, and only attended to when failures/deficits in such feminine care result in damaged adult behaviors, attitudes, or transgressions. The point is that certain degrees of excess—the kind we have seen in Donald Trump—actually require a rather complete absence of the Jungian feminine: the caring for or about the other. We will return to this later, but for the purpose of an illustration of this first definition of excess as "outrageousness," no further elaboration is needed.

Let us go now then to the second and third definitions of excess for what they also bring in terms of explaining how Trump stands as a culminating figure of America's illnesses of excess (which is to say that it is not simply all about him, however much he says so!).

### 20th English Definition of Excess as "Eliminating The Position of": The Verb

The second definition of excess brings us up to more current times. In 1971, a new definition emerged and moved "excess" from being considered primarily in terms of the individual to considerations concerning the group.

Whereas the earlier definition of excess is most commonly used as an adjective, this newer definition appeared in the English language as a transitive verb meaning: "to eliminate the position of," as in, "We 'excessed' several teachers because of budgetary cutbacks."[5] This new bead of meaning added to excess implicitly includes within it the complexity of group dynamics. While every larger social structure makes some judgments regarding who and what is essential, and who and what are "in excess" to be eliminated or "excessed," *who* to "excess" is of course much more ethically problematic than "what" ought to be excessed for the welfare of any social group.

This definition of excess emerged in the late twentieth century during the baby boomer period of multiple social movements such as civil rights, feminism, and gay rights in America, where who has been, is, and will be "excessed" from inclusion in the social and legal netting was being actively questioned. Our own founding Puritans were in a sense "excessed" from their European countries—perhaps giving Americans a special unconscious relationship to this particular meaning of excess.

Certainly, the most egregious "excessing" has been America's appropriation of native American lands by European settlers, concurrent with the enslavement and exploitation of African people to build this nation, followed again by "excessing" them through Jim Crow laws, voter suppression, and outright terror tactics. Similarly, even though a 2015 US Supreme Court decision affirmed legal marriage equality for the "excessed" homosexual group, the reality is that it remains a contentious issue of fundamentalist Christian religious debate today—where some insist that God prescribes such people be "excessed" from the social structure of recognition, rights, and humanity's care. (And in fact, with the repeal of abortion rights in the Dobbs 2022 decision, Supreme Court Justice Thomas explicitly named gay rights and access to contraception for repeal consideration.)

This second aspect of excess has been demonstrated and repeatedly endorsed by Trump in hate speech and "exclusionary" policies—beginning with announcing his candidacy by calling for the elimination of Mexican immigrants—or perhaps more correctly, all that is non-white. Tapping into a pre-existing cultural tap root, his verbal utterances resulted in a significant upsurge in this kind of excessing, demonstrated by the dramatic increase in "hate" crimes soon after his assumption of the presidency.[6] The number of hate groups also increased during the Trump administration.[7]

It is easy to see how Trump embodies these two meanings of excess, but it is, in fact, a third definition of excess that he enacts repeatedly, and that has been, and continues to be, the most destructive—pulsing and metastasizing through major swaths of our citizenry—and being demonstrated explicitly on January 6, 2021. It is this version of excess that has made us as a culture particularly vulnerable to the emergence of a dangerously demagogic leader such as Trump—because while Trump may be the pinnacle, he was not the originator. So, stay with us here re: this third definition of excess.

### In 14th Century Late Latin, the Word Was "Excessus": A Departure, a Going Beyond the Bounds of Reason or Beyond the Subject[8]

We are focused here on elaborating an aspect of what is "beyond the subject." What does this mean and why is it important? No matter how articulate any of us becomes, our actual experience often exceeds language—is in "excess" of the words we use to describe that experience—in a word, ineffable. Our human narrative of learned words and images only partially expresses the thoughts and feelings we experience. At the foundation of each human being then, there is the enduring reality that there will always be a degree of excess—something beyond what any word or image can scoop up and express. For example, when we say, "I love ..." or "I hate ...", how much is in the word and how much more is outside it? We all count on both the inside and outside of language to get our message across!

So—and this is the important part—this excess beyond what language can hold has unique effects, indeed parallel with the power of words and images to express our experience. This excess beyond verbal representation is at times something we are conscious of, but it is also at times unconscious. We may be aware or unaware in speaking that we are including both parts. The part that cannot be captured in words nonetheless moves us daily, and profoundly, in our thoughts, feelings, attitudes, decisions, and actions. All those bits of excess beyond words push and pull us toward or away from action—sometimes before we are even consciously aware of the push and pull. Perhaps only later (and sometimes never) do we retrospectively more fully understand that decision or that action in words. We "fell in love with" this person; we "knew" this was the house for us, or Trump's "will be wild!" in calling an insurrection into life.

At the same time, from another vantage point, we also commonly chase those excess bits, as if we could grab what exceeds our words to complete ourselves. In essence, we strive to fill in a feeling of *missing* or *lacking something* in ourselves. We do this sometimes through pursuing the fantasy elements in relationships, but also via overeating, sex, religious fervor, money, drugs, rock & roll. We all experience this. Sometimes in that unachievable chase to complete ourselves—or to fill in the gaps that language leaves in us—we can also tell ourselves stories of how others are to blame for our not being able to achieve our own completion (for example, the marchers in Charlottesville, VA chanting "Jews will not replace us").

It is this third facet of the word "excess"—that which is left over beyond words—that Trump intentionally uses, both in what he says and what he leaves out. He is "tremendous" at this (as he might say himself!). Many have pointed out that Trump's destructive use of excess in the realm of language impacts the very institutions of our democracy. It is, actually, much worse than that. It is an attack on the very denotational and connotational structures of language itself, and therefore an attack upon civilization.

So, let's examine just a few examples of Trump's excesses in his use of language, both in what he says and in what he leaves out, because it is a crucial lesson in the power and frailty of language as humanity's foundational building material.

### Excessive Things Spoken

There are things that Trump says and means explicitly that are excessive and destructive. For example, he clearly meant: "I'm automatically attracted to beautiful women—I just start kissing them. It's like a magnet" when he spoke his own emotional truth here about women and their place as servants of his desire. And as misogynistic as these words were (and some actually thought it might sink his candidacy), it did not sink him, and in fact, more white women voted for him in 2020 than in 2016! On the other hand, these words also inspired the largest single day of protest ever in America by women and their supporters the day after his 2017 inauguration!

He also clearly meant these potent words: "I alone can fix it," professing a belief in his own narcissistic omniscience and omnipotence. This hubris in essence declares, "I name it and it will happen." It is, of course, patently false, but imbues him with a god-like mien that perverts the truth of his human limitations, and causes some to assert faith in this hubris. Another statement from 2016 was more threatening, telling, and ultimately manifested in a manner on January 6, 2021: his statement on January 23, 2016 that "I could stand in the middle of Fifth Avenue and shoot somebody and I wouldn't lose any voters, ok."

Sometimes Trump also says things that he means, which violate material truth, but which he attempts to make true through "magical thinking"—as in, "I can only lose the election if it is rigged"—even when many of his own administration and allies told him after the 2020 election that he had actually lost. In this perversion of truth, he has dragged many, many people into a delusional fantasy with him. (And in this sense, we can all be vulnerable to fantasies that promise to fill in something lost or missing in us rather than accepting a loss and reorganizing ourselves to incorporate this reality.)

### Excessive Things Not Spoken

Sometimes Trump's excess is in what he does not say. A wizard of the perversion of language, Trump uses phrases and incomplete sentences that he leaves intentionally vague to be filled in by his audience, with projected negative or positive feelings or thoughts from ordinary people who are making their own efforts to fill in missing or incomplete bits of themselves. "Big protest in DC on January 6th. Be there, will be wild." Such words do not capture, nor are they ever intended to capture, a truthful meaning. Trump intentionally, perhaps—intuitively most certainly—makes the most out of this meaning of excess by his very particular use of language. Trump perverts language at its core. For what language can do at its best is to gather up experience and express it meaningfully to others. When language can do this, it facilitates human relationships, enhances creativity, and helps to minimize destructive human behavior by "talking" through feelings and ideas. When language loses its connection to truth, this positive and creative power of language erodes. Lies erode, and ultimately destroy, the meaning of words themselves.

Early in the Trump administration, Kellyanne Conway's declaration of "alternative facts" aided and abetted the widening of these destructive effects. Fox News and other internet-based groups took up this practice, normalizing it over four years.[9] These destructive effects became even more evident during the aftermath of the 2020 election, with Trump's failure to accept the reality of his loss, even after "reasonable" legal protests—63 lawsuits in all—were exhausted or rejected by the courts. His delusion fomented and fueled the January 6 insurrection. And the Republican Party, as if caught up in a spell, joined in with their refusal to stand up for democracy's hallowed structures. The Congressional January 6th Hearing's report has illuminated all of this.

Trump's use of language has been primitive and often destructive in tone and in intention. Trump has carried on an unrelenting attack on the gathering and expressive capacities of language itself. In fact, linguists have commented that Trump exhibits the most primitive language usage of any of the last 15 presidents. They have noted that as the presidential challenges accumulated beyond his abilities, Trump's language stretched toward more and more aggressive words and "force" symbols.[10] Trump shows in technicolor how the inherent power of language can be perverted, emptied, and even rendered dead. When words are not grounded in material truths—making words "not really matter"—the spaces between the letters and words themselves degrade into the brutality of the purely instinctual world, as we have unfortunately all witnessed.

Language is not simply a communication tool, but one of the most crucial building materials human beings have in society. But language itself can be damaged and rendered inert. Even though the radio launch of hate speech by Rush Limbaugh of the 1980s and the explicit weaponizing of language by Newt Gingrich in the 1990s preceded Trump, a different magnitude of reach and impact occurs when that speech is coming from the President of the United States.

In the misuse and abuse of language, the amount of what is "in excess" beyond the words themselves can be vastly increased. As this happens, the excess then can begin to turn in on itself, moving into a toxic range, pushing human beings more and more toward "acting things out" versus "talking things through." We all witnessed the open call for violence against selected others on January 6, 2021 (the cries of the crowd to "Hang Mike Pence!"), coupled with the aggression against the institutions of American government itself.

**The Bottom Line**

To this point, then, Trump can be seen as an iconic figure embodying the multiple meanings of excess—excesses building in America for decades. Two of the three definitions of excess—(1) outrageousness itself and (2) the act of eliminating the position of someone or something(s)—are glaringly evident in Trump's language and agenda. Concerning the third definition of excess—that which exists outside the limits of language per se but is very "real" in its effects—this aspect, perhaps remains the most culturally dangerous.

In Chapter 2, both image and words were used to create a felt sense of the unconscious as it lives at the fluid foundation of every human being. In the next chapter, we look more closely and evocatively at "the feminine principle" lying at humanity's psychic foundations, to see how the twinning of the unconscious with the feminine can occur. We also observe how there has been a long-standing patriarchal diminishment, if not attempted erasure, of both the feminine principle and the unconscious. It is well past time that as a culture we become aware of that pernicious influence in our culture, and to get about the work of changing it.

## Notes

1 *Merriam-Webster Dictionary* (2020). G. & C. Merriam Co.
2 Just one prominent example of Trump excess: using the DC Trump hotel for government events with proceeds going to the Trump business entity, as well as overcharging the secret service for hotel rooms.
3 See Jung (1969) *Archetypes and the Collective Unconscious*, Collected Works of C. G. Jung, Vol. 9 (Part 1) (G. Adler, & R. F. C. Hull, eds), Princeton University Press; and Polly Young-Eisendrath's (2004) *Subject to Change: Jung, Gender, and Subjectivity in Psychoanalysis*. Brunner-Routledge; as well as her contextual work with Dawson (2010) *The Cambridge companion to Jung. Cambridge University Press*, putting Jungian notions in play with object relations and relational theory use of these terms. See also relational school theorists Adrienne Harris, Ken Corbett, Jessica Benjamin, Dianne Elise for their interesting work in this realm.
4 There have been different feminist critiques of essentialist cast definitions of both masculine and feminine principles which inform our framing here of emphasizing the psychological—but without throwing out contributing biological elements and also not making biology determinative nor prescriptive.
5 *Merriam-Webster Dictionary* (2020). G. & C. Merriam Co.
6 Actual US hate crimes were up again in 2022, into a fourth straight year, according to new data from the Center for the Study of Hate & Extremism (CSHE) (Farivar, 2022).
7 See the 2019 article "Hate Groups Reach Record High" by the Southern Poverty Law Center; hate groups increased during three years of Trump's term, going down then in 2020.
8 *Merriam-Webster Dictionary* (2020). G. & C. Merriam Co.
9 Fox news persisted in lying about voting machine irregularities, resulting in a $1.6bn suit by Dominion brought against Fox Corp. Words do matter!
10 In a comparative analysis of 15 US Presidents using the Flesch-Kincaid linguistic scale for level of language usage, Trump came last—the most primitive speaker. See Osnos (2020) "Pulling our politics back from the brink" in *The New Yorker*.

## References

Farivar, M. (2022). US hate crimes rise during first half of 2022. VOA News, August 23. https://www.voanews.com/a/us-hate-crimes-rise-during-first-half-of-2022-/6713791.html

Government Accountability Office (GAO) (2019). Presidential travel: Secret Service and DOD need to ensure that expenditure reports are prepared and submitted to Congress. GAO-19-178. Washington, DC: US Government Printing Office.

House of Representatives, Congress. (2022). Final report of the Select Committee to investigate the January 6th attack on the United States Capitol. GovInfo, December 21. https://www.govinfo.gov/app/details/GPO-J6-REPORT/context

Johnstone, L. (2019). Tracking President Trump's visits to Trump properties. NBC News, October 22. https://www.nbcnews.com/politics/donald-trump/how-much-time-trump-spends-trump-properties-mar-lago-n753366

Jung, C. G. (1969). *Collected Works of C.G. Jung, Volume 9, Part 1: Archetypes and the Collective Unconscious* (G. Adler & R. F. C. Hull, Eds.). Princeton University Press. http://www.jstor.org/stable/j.ctt5hhrnk

*Merriam-Webster Dictionary* (2020). G. & C. Merriam Co.

Osnos, E. (2020). Pulling our politics back from the brink. *The New Yorker*, November 9. https://www.newyorker.com/magazine/2020/11/16/pulling-our-politics-back-from-the-brink

Young-Eisendrath, P. (2004). *Subject to Change: Jung, Gender, and Subjectivity in Psychoanalysis*. Brunner-Routledge.

Young-Eisendrath, P., & Dawson, T. (eds) (2010). *The Cambridge Companion to Jung*. Cambridge University Press.

Chapter 4

# Indispensable Invisible Foundations

## Our Feminine Roots

There is yet another aspect of the word "excess" that we need to examine together, one that points to "negative" excess—the *absence* of something *essential* or crucial. In these next few pages, we investigate the psychological and foundational aspects of becoming human, which are rooted in the ministrations of maternal/feminine care and guardianship over the smallest and most powerless among us—our children. Without this thread, Trump, the man, and Trump, as symbol, remain inscrutable.

Much goes into the formation of an adult person. We have highlighted that there are deep layers of the unconscious psyche that are formed very early on in identity development. We've also pointed out how much our first few years of life—always still alive within the unconscious parts of our mind—are crucial to later versions of the self. As in all civilized societies, America puts its money where its mouth is—and where its values are. It is notable, then, that as a culture, America has largely financially discounted the crucial importance of care for early childhood. America lives with a checkered relationship to early childhood, perhaps reflecting a willful blindness—to the importance of the feminine function in terms of seeding and nurturing the human unconscious. This is unassailably evident in its structures and glaring funding gaps. America is the only country, for instance, of 41 OECD countries, without a national statutory paid maternity, paternity or parental leave plan.[1] Further, there has been no ongoing government or business investment in a viable infrastructure for day-to-day childcare for parent workers. (This, according to the Organization for Economic Cooperation and Development data from the 41 OECD countries and European Union.)

### Foundations May Be Invisible, But They Keep a House From Falling in on Itself

We know from decades of developmental research that a psychologically stable self is only constructed within a safe and reliable relationship.[2] This process depends on having an emotionally invested and attuned-enough other to provide this safety and reliability both at birth and during the first

DOI: 10.4324/9781032677309-5

few years. When these things are in place, the self can take root and develop in health. Elemental to that rooting is the empathic receiving of a baby's instinctual needs and emotional passions and the help to temper and transform them to become a civilized person in that society. As a child moves from infancy to toddlerhood to becoming a talking child, language itself becomes instrumental in emotional expression. "Use your words," we say. Language, in addition to helping to modify feelings, thoughts, and behavior, also erects and holds the barrier (we call it the repressive barrier) against deeply instinctual and unmodulated animalistic impulses—especially very destructive impulses. Remember that bottom ocean layer of the unconscious?

So, how do any of us develop human empathy and personal restraint? Here's how. Initially, the baby perceives the mother (or maternal caretaker) to be an omnipotent and benign other, someone who absorbs and transforms all and anything that the child sends her way. And hopefully, at first, this is true enough. In "good enough" circumstances, a baby in face-to-face encounters sees another who welcomes them, is invested in them, and tends to their aliveness—while that other all the while mirrors in their own face and being something of that baby's own particular aliveness back to them. It is reasonable to think that at the level of the first foundations of the human psyche, a trace is laid—in the baby's evolving psychic structure—of a fundamental sense of human responsibility for another. So, begin the first fragile tendrils of an ethic of love.[3]

In time, with "good enough" parenting, the maturing baby comes to realize that mother too has her limits, can in fact be hurt, and that the baby has, within themselves, their own capacity to be destructive as well as loving. Here's an example: the birth of a sibling can elicit intense feelings of "like me!" but also rivalrous feelings to "get rid of the intruder!" Degrees of attraction and love are accompanied by rivalry and quasi-murderous wishes. The child's psychic task becomes one of leaning into the empathy based in similarity—"they are like me, but different"—while pulling back the aggression and murderous fantasies that threaten the sibling. For all this to evolve into a working internal structure in the child, the mother or caregiver must offer loving support and the threat of withdrawal of love in the face of emergent aggression toward the sibling. This "law of the mother"[4] establishes both a mark of difference from and similarity to others, and the fact that more than one can be loved (starting with mother). This serial experience becomes foundational to the development of the evolving self, in which responsibility toward others moves a child forward in an ethic of love.

So, there is within most of us a deep psychic structure consisting of a well of empathy and recognition of a similar "other"—where difference can be held and valued and destructive impulses held in check. This process takes place primarily in the time before we can speak or fully understand—when language is experienced as an emotionally felt, sensorially based experience (see Chapter 2).

Later versions of this deep structure take their place in language—in our ethical codes and written societal laws. There is also a vertical axis of generational difference establishing separate and different privileges and responsibilities by generation (for example, the taboo of incest, and murder). This is what culture emphasizes as most important, reflected in our written codes of law. And yet, the first level of individual difference and limit on aggression toward an other actually begins in the "law of the mother"—the unwritten space of the maternal feminine—operating on the horizontal axis between individuals of the same generation. The first trace of the development of psychic structure is there. Even though the patriarchal order of most cultures inscribes the "rule of law" as the privileged currency of the masculine—and asserts claims to civilization as if it exists only in the terms of "the law of the father," it could be said that it is the deeper structure of "the law of the mother" that precedes and undergirds this law. In fact, that is part of what has enabled the international community of democratic nations to support their sibling, Ukraine, against a bigger neighboring bully![5]

So, what happens when a receptive, holding, transformative caretaking other fails, is missing, or is too inconsistently present in those early years? In other words, what happens when there is absence—a kind of *negative excess*," perhaps? The answer is this: there will be compromises within the self of that person and compromises in relation to others. The compromises of the self will include instability, insecurity, and immaturity. And, when the self is unstable, there can be chronic use of the primitive defenses of an immature self—defenses such as infantile narcissism, grandiosity, retaliatory persistent bullying, projection, reversal, negation. There can also be chronic fragility and brittleness.

In relation to others, where the good-enough maternal support is missing in this process, deficits in empathy can occur. Rivalry and defensive independence can lose their balance—often becoming overlain in later development with unbridled aggression. Distortions and breakthroughs of our crucial repressive barrier—which keeps the more animalistic impulses within at bay—can occur to a much greater extent and with greater frequency. Often, the center of the rule of language does not hold, so those words inside our heads we usually say to ourselves that help suppress or manage the most destructive forces within us don't work or are simply not there. Recall, for instance, Trump's motoric imitation of a disabled person in his campaign for the presidency.

One more important thing is this: one of the basic tenets in the field of psychology is that "being" must precede "doing." The "being" time is when a mother absorbs and transforms what comes her way.[6] So, when the ongoing conditions for good-enough "continuity of being" are lacking very early on in life, there can develop instead an over-reliance on "doing" to compensate—if a child has the inherent intellectual capacity to do so. For those locked within this compensatory "doing" mode, any sense of loss or "losing" can be experienced as an annihilation of their very being. This, as you can imagine, would be terrifying and unacceptable—to anyone. How can anyone possibly tolerate annihilation? This is one way to understand Trump's delusional rejection of his election loss. His effort to pervert language at its foundational level, by lying his way out of a political defeat, is because defeat for him is not just losing—it threatens an annihilation of his very being. Thus, he simply cannot abide being a "loser."

As psychologists, we understand the Trump presidency as a four-year, slow-motion illustration of what happens within an adult human when one's foundational sense of self is quite compromised. Even more disturbing is the fact that this disturbing exhibition continues to command attention on the national stage. Trump brings our attention to what are—and are not—optimal conditions for establishing a stable self and a self that "plays well with others." He in fact displayed, over four years and now beyond, how very much our first few years of life—always still alive within the unconscious parts of our mind—are crucial to later versions of one's conscious self. Trump's chronic use of the more primitive defenses of an immature self all speak to a less than stable self.

Many Americans were shocked for quite some time that an adult—especially on such a public stage as the presidency—would talk and act as Trump did toward others. Trump was a "cosplay"—an enacted version of an American president. When he did not "grow into" or "rise to the role of" president, shock moved into anxiety and fear among multiple governmental and military staff, and then it moved into real defensive strategies by them for management and self-protection. This is fact we have heard much more about after the 2020 election.[7] Post-presidency, each time more evidence of unlawful action is discovered, there is the unwelcome realization that his verbal intentions and actions were more destructive than many could ever have imagined a US president enacting!

The Trump presidency and the years since have possibly been the best conceivable presentation of why we need a cultural shift with respect to the unseen and undervalued function of the feminine and the maternal in our national life. It has also been a four-plus year presentation of the layered nature of the human psyche, and what it feels and sounds like when someone speaks and acts from their more primitive and unconsciously organized self. Mary Trump, Donald Trump's niece and a psychologist, has offered a poignant and searing analysis of the missing and askew feminine elements in Donald Trump's family history.[8] Thus we have seen on our most public world stage what happens when the maternal parental function has been significantly compromised in a child's early life, and an exaggerated identification with an immature masculine parental function takes its place.

In addition to the noted individual failures of empathy in Trump's personal and professional relationships—which reflect these early deficits writ large—we must note two massive empathic failures at the level of the society/group. Trump's inability to empathize or to see beyond the "bad PR" for himself at the inception of the Covid pandemic resulted in hundreds of thousands of deaths—because of his primitive use of denial, the suppression of scientific advice, his misinformation, and the politicization of masks and vaccines—even as he availed himself of state-of-the-art medical treatments during his own illness.[9]

And, on the level of Planet Earth, Trump's failure of empathy led to his immediate withdrawal from the Paris Climate Accord—citing American economic concerns. This position—one held by too many nations, for way too long—spoke not only to his deficits in empathy, but to another serious deficit within the realm of the feminine function in human development. Climate change deniers/diminishers, like Trump, are operating like infants at a certain level—continuing to see Mother Earth as an omnipotent resource versus as a precious support of life that can be damaged, too. Economic considerations ultimately mean nothing when there is no more planet—which the young activist Greta Thunberg has forcefully expressed to the world. Thus, we witness on a global stage what happens when the feminine/parental function is significantly missing or askew.

Through developmental description offered in this chapter, it is hoped that the often invisible but indispensable human foundation, resting as it does on the feminine principle and function, might become more visible and more undeniable in its consequences—positive and negative—for a person's unfolding life.

Despite the clear deficits in the feminine principle in Trump the man, there is a hopeful aspect to this paroxysm of excess which we have experienced over decades, with Trump as its capstone figure. A more hopeful rendering comes from that parallactic view, mentioned previously, of the unfolding arc of excess. America appears to be approaching a "tipping point"[10] —where a newly emergent consciousness of our doomed love affair with excess is a sign that the culture is moving toward a needed integration of a big, but very "slow idea." This concerns the place of the unconscious—and unconscious influences in the group's as well as the nation's future choices. Pursuant to this path of more psychic integration, we have identified a perhaps crucial orienting axis for twenty-first-century feminism—one that issues a different kind of "call to arms"—anticipating and leaning into this tipping point. In the next chapter we take a closer look at this "parallactic view" of excess and its potential emergent influence.

## Notes

1  Also of interest, the Society for Human Resource Management (SHRM) reported in 2017 that 60% of employers offer 12 weeks of maternity leave; 33% offer

longer leaves. In Scandanavia, parents are entitled to a total of 12 months' leave in connection with the birth and after the birth.

2  Start with Bowlby (2005) and then Fonagy (2001) on attachment and then mentalization (2002). See also Daniel Stern (2000).
Worth noting that while Winnicott described, across his work, the crucial significance of relational matrix of infancy, Fonagy (and his colleagues) have devoted themselves to fleshing that territory out, so to speak, through research that has precipitated names for functions therein.

3  See Winnicott's multiple papers (1990).

4  See Mitchel (2023) about this neglected level of development. Helping to explain the confusion of patriarchy perhaps—see Lacan's essays "The signification of the phallus" and "The function and field of speech and language in psychoanalysis" in *Ecrit* (1977) for exploration of how the penis, as a concrete "thing", can become over-valued in that it becomes associated with the psychic movement from operating only in the instinctual world of "the thing" itself, to the world of representations and symbols for "the thing," which is where human expressiveness and creativity take flight. Or, as Carl Jung once said, "The penis is just a phallic symbol." Freud's premise was that in the unconscious of the (always assuming male as prototype) infant, the mother is assumed to actually have a penis, but when the infant discovers she does not, or is missing one, instead of seeing she has "something different"—and therefore is not really missing something—the infant now sees femaleness as standing for lack, while maleness carries the illusion then to have it all. And yet, actually, something is both gained and lost for all human infants in the process of entering the symbolic representational world.
A great deal of the early human infant journey is concerned with this leap from a purely biological destiny, to entering into symbolization (images and language) as foundational to the human condition. But an unconscious association of penis as having it all—when really the penis is simple a good example of a concrete thing that we can imagine missing or taken off, easily lends itself to being represented by a symbol. Confusion of biology and symbol have abounded—resulting in a spinning out into over-privileged patriarchal orders of societies accompanied by gender inequity and abuse.

5  It was likely also a part of Colonel Vindeman's drawing the line on Trump's attempt to extort the president of Ukraine to lie about Hunter Biden. It was not simply the rule of law that said no, it was also an empathic resonance with a younger sibling being bullied by a bigger or older sibling. Also, beyond the scope of this presentation to differentiate, Lacan's "law of the father" implies the presence of "a third" during infancy via bringing language into the dyad, as well as her own desire for someone or something beyond that dyad (that of an actual father or another). This in essence is before the period we usually think of as the Oedipal time, when the purpose here is to highlight the privileging of the masculine and conscious laws.

6  See pediatrician and psychoanalyst Donald Winnicott (1970) and other writings for an elaboration on this topic. Winnicott painstakingly lays out the early realm of the mother-child relationship that fosters the development of a healthy self. See also Quatman (2020) for a very readable amplification of a dozen of his most important papers.

7  For example, see Bolton (2020).

8  See Mary Trump (2022) or any of a number of her publicly available inter-
   views on cable news for a unique and useful perspective on Trump's continuing
   functioning.
9  Again, Mary Trump has put her finger on the unnecessary loss of American life
   due to Trump policies and wondered if this is not a genocide.
10  See Gladwell (2002) for a full discussion of this concept.

## References

Bolton, J. (2020). *The Room Where It Happened*. Simon Schuster.

Bowlby, J. (2005). *A Secure Base: Clinical Applications of Attachment Theory*.
   Routledge (original work published 1988).

Fonagy, P. (2001). *Attachment and psychoanalysis*. Routledge.

Fonagy, P., Gergely, G., & Jurist, E. L. (eds) (2018). *Affect Regulation, Mentalization
   and the Development of the Self*. Routledge.

Gladwell, M. (2002). *The Tipping Point*. Little Brown & Company.

Lacan, J. (1977). *Ecrits: A Selection* (trans. Alan Sheridan). W.W. Norton & Company.

Mitchel, J. (2023). *Fratriarchy: The Sibling Trauma and the Law of the Mother*.
   Routledge.

Quatman, T. (2020). *Accessing the Clinical Genius of Winnicott*. Routledge.

Stern, D. (2000). *The Interpersonal World of the Infant*. Basic Books.

Trump, M. (2022). *Too Much and Never Enough: How My Family Produced the
   Most Dangerous Man in the World*. Simon & Schuster.

Winnicott, D. W. (1970). *Playing and Reality*. Basic Books.

Winnicott, D. W. (1990). *The Maturational Processes and the Facilitating
   Environment: Studies in the Theory of Emotional Development*. Karnac Books.

# Chapter 5

# Excess as Access

## Foreshadowing Unconscious Knowledge

Trump's ascension to the presidency *and* his continued presence on the national scene afford a third perspective beyond the split characterizations of messiah versus destroyer that are so often ascribed to him. It is this third parallactic perspective that caught our attention. Certainly, Trump does represent the apogee of the several decades of accumulating American excesses—the erosion of the middle class, the skyrocketing of CEO salaries, the recasting of the American Dream from a happy life to a super-wealthy life, the elevation of Ivy League university admissions to a national obsession (to be pursued, and even cheated for), the increase of mass shootings in schools and public locations, the spiraling of the national opioid crisis that appears unstoppable.[1] There has also emerged a kind of "lottery" mentality that finds more and more people looking for the BIG win, either via the lottery itself or via choosing the right company (with stock options), with the hope of being bought out by a yet-bigger company, all leading to the holy grail of extraordinary individual wealth—currently a common American fantasy.[2]

But perhaps Trump, without his conscious intention, may be freighting yet another aspect of excess unbeknown to him. That is, "excess" presenting a message to be deciphered. To "presage" is to foreshadow something, as in, to hint about something that is to come.[3] The directional valence of that foreshadowing message may be positive or negative. It can be a herald or a harbinger.[4]

What can be said about excess as a directional message? Excesses in the individual psyche, when recognized and read as unconscious knowledge waiting to be deciphered, can be useful information—to understand what has been going on, and to guide conscious decision making going forward. At the group or societal level, the same may be true. But one must be alert enough to read the signs. For example, it's easy enough in retrospect to read the foreshadowing of the rise of Nazism in pre-Second World War Germany, but was there enough cultural alertness to read the road signs of the accumulating excesses in advance, to prevent the cataclysm that was wrought by Adolph Hitler? Clearly not.

DOI: 10.4324/9781032677309-6

So, back to America, excess, and foreshadowing. The word "excess" itself became more prominent in our cultural discourse during the first two decades of the twenty-first century. For example, in a quick search of book titles from 2000 to 2015—as one simple measure of America's attention—more than 200 books were published with the word "excess" in their title.

Here is an interesting dozen:

> *The road of excess: The history of writers on drugs (2005)*
> *Excess: Anti-consumerism in the West (2009)*
> *The culture of excess: How America lost self-control and why we need to re-define success (2009)*
> *Gender and the poetics of excess (2009)*
> *Getting rid of excess baggage in our lives (2010)*
> *Luxury fever: Weighing the costs of excess (2010)*
> *The economics of excess: Addictions, indulgences, and social policy (2011)*
> *We have met the enemy: Self-control in the age of excess (2011)*
> *The issues of American excess: Temptation: finding self-control in an age of excess (2011)*
> *The arrogant leader: Dealing with the excesses of power (2012)*
> *Eat to live: Recipes to lose belly fat excess (2013)*

As noted at the opening of this chapter, the phenomenon of excess in the decades since the 1980s increased across multiple life venues. Apropos to Oscar Wilde's quip, "Nothing succeeds like excess," the pursuit of excess came to be a stance many in America agreed with. Wrapped up with excess in a multitude of ways, it could be said that for children born in the 1980s and going forward, the notion of "excess" has essentially been "the water they swim in."

### Renewal through Re-inscription

Psychoanalyst Jacques Lacan noted that there are times in society when a particular word can become reinscribed—re-written—within the cultural lexicon; in other words, re-established or re-named in a new way or context. The word "excess"—our American obsession with excess of all kinds and, in particular, the *insistence* of this phenomenon in our culture—has seemingly become such a word.

The relationship between a word and what it stands for is not fixed; it is mutable. It is in relationship to the other signifiers in a sentence that it will exhibit its full meaning. The map of social meanings we live in also moves and shifts—over and in time. The assumed meaning of a word can shift and/ or add to itself over time—as was the case with the word "excess" in 1970s, adding the meaning of "to eliminate" someone from society's net of social care and legal protection. Additional meanings for a word or signifier can occur when a society is in the process of developing something new or different for itself. This re-inscription, or reconsidering of the word "excess," serves the psychological function of something new becoming possible in society in a way not imagined before.[5]

If the unconscious messages contained in our cultural pursuit of excess can be interpreted, faced, and psychically integrated, a positive result might occur. In our current cultural state, however, the foreshadowed message(s) of excess carry a more foreboding and ominous implication. When unconscious knowledge is available, but is culturally ignored, we are consigned as a society to remain in its negatively valanced emotional orbit.

In its most positive vein, per the title of this chapter, "Excess *can be* access." It can provide insight to claim as our own through understanding and interpretation of excess, and also to influence the creating of structural remedies for our profligate social problems. Although Biden/Harris won more votes "by a lot" as Trump claimed for himself, Trump did receive over *70 million votes*! And the insurrection of January 6, 2021 offers further evidence that potential violent excesses remain insufficiently interpreted and integrated into our national group psyche. That demonstration of excess *in violence*, and in the threat of civil war following the 2022 FBI search of Mar-a Largo, stand as harbingers of more future violence, if useful interpretations and actions cannot be made and directed toward those 70 million voters (not to mention the millions who did not even vote, thinking their vote probably did not matter!). It is unclear how many repetitions of violent excesses (in words and deeds) are needed before the information that may be accessible through insightful, psychological interpretation can be read with sufficient psychological understanding to be translated into adequate action and social policy aimed toward those 70 million people.[6]

Centuries ago, unconscious knowledge was seen as a valid and operative contribution to ancient rulers' policy-making in the form of their being attentive to their own dreams and then having them interpreted by trusted wise persons in their court. America has eschewed such unconscious messages, whether gleaned from dreams, or in this context, manifested in the multiple accumulating instances of cultural excess. This turning away is in large part due to our overvaluing and privileging of the conscious mind versus the deeper unconscious levels of the mind as the only part of the human psyche that really matters. So, what this really means then is that we are only responsible for the conscious contents of our minds!

Yes, there are those Freudian slips of tongue and the "forgetting" of things that Western societies have taken as their token cultural acknowledgments of the unconscious, but, as a living reality to be factored into significant individual or group decision making, *it's not happening*! To give the unconscious the place it deserves in human functioning and for people in general to *own it*, something must substantially shift in the way our culture thinks. Andrew Yang's presidential slogan—Make America Think Harder—more accurately needs to be: Help America Think Differently.

Inscribing a new meaning of excess as a "foreshadower" would encourage curiosity and perhaps, even, a seeking of messages-in-waiting. "Excess" defined as a stimulus or a foreshadowing would center us as a society upon the decoding or interpreting unconscious messages carried within our glaring excesses. Responding to and reading the past and present excesses could impel a reaching toward a new cultural integration, wherein the dynamic unconscious could become a part of our everyday understanding of what it means to be human, and how society at large might function differently. It would also comprise a potent push for the ushering in of a new era, where the "ethos of care" could better take its proper place alongside what has been America's "ethic of individual freedom." As such, it would impact how "fairness" or "equity" could be looked at differently, as well as how it might be calibrated differently in social policy terms.

A question hovering is this: can the work of feminism in this century make use of "*excess as access*" and lean strongly into moving toward this integration of the unconscious mind as foundational in the human experience? In doing so, we envision that the roots of unconscious sexism could be directly addressed—as the unconscious would become a factor always to be considered in any decisions regarding meaningful action. So, rather than feminism's only "looking up" to break glass and sexist ceilings, might we imagine the added necessity of a looking down or looking elsewhere toward the unconscious elements of human life—especially—but not solely—those contributing to acquisitiveness, sexism, and racism—but really all the "isms"—that selectively de-humanize others. It is with just such a "leaning into" in mind that a "call to arms" for twenty-first-century feminism ultimately came forward after the 2016 election loss of Hillary Clinton—only to continue to accrue and deepen—across the time of Trump's presidency into our present moment. Within these years, a "cultural ripeness" has also been building, with additive gravitational force, cresting toward a "tipping point."

So, now going forward, cultural ripeness and the tipping point phenomenon become the focus of the next chapter.

## Notes

1  See Slosar (2009) who looks closely at this phenomenon in America. Additional works speak to various facets of this—Paarlberg (2015) looks at overconsumption of fuel and food. Twenge and Donnelly's (2016) work on students' reasons for going to college revealing increased emphasis on extrinsic reasons ("to make more money"). Hayes (2013) points out how America's meritocracy is inherently flawed, fueling inequality and excess. See Piketty's (2014) nuanced discussion of financial equity and other economic factors around this trend.

2  The magical solution inherent in "hitting the lottery" in reality, or by working in a company that "hits it big", can perhaps be better empathized within an environment of increased mass shootings—in public places—and in school settings where citizens, especially children, should be safe. Increased incidence of anxiety and depression among children, especially adolescents, has only been magnified by the impact of the pandemic.

The other side of the lottery dream of instant wealth is noted by the Center for Disease Control and Prevention that suicides increased 37% in America from 2000 to 2018, then dipped for two years, and then returned to the 2018 peak. Also, according to an American Psychological Association Emerging Trends report (Spiner, 2022), the number of trained child therapists and school psychologists is woefully inadequate to the burgeoning mental health crises of children. Meanwhile, the mental health needs of adults dealing with multi-faceted effects of a two-plus years pandemic are also in excess of clinicians' capacity to meet them—with therapists everywhere reporting being swamped with virtually no openings in any timely manner.

3  See *Merriam-Webster* on "foreshadow" as a transitive verb. Authors give thanks to Susan Ovrovitz, PhD for suggesting the word "foreshadow" for the working out of our thoughts.

4  In Joseph Campbell's (1968) exploration of Western Greek mythology, Hermes (called Mercury by the Romans) was the son of Maia and Zeus and designated by Zeus as the herald of the gods—heralding messages across the border from the gods to humanity. Hermes' name is rooted in the Greek word for a pile of stones which is how early land borders were marked. His union with Aphrodite bearing Hermaphrodite (of both sexes) and Persephone (living part-time in both conscious and unconscious worlds) were both also complex border-focused and border crossing figures.

5  See Lacan (1997) Seminar III, Seminar IV (2021), Seminar XI (2018) especially.

6  See Nusbaum's (2018) very accessible book that draws on both philosophy and work of analyst Donald Winnicott to propose governmental approaches to address citizens' primitive fears of survival and security that could be addressed programmatically.

## References

Campbell, J. (1968). *The Hero with a Thousand Faces*. Pantheon Books (first published 1949).

Center for Disease Control and Prevention (2023). Suicide Data and Statistics Report, updated May 5.

Hayes, C. (2013). *Twilight of the Elites*. Crown Publishing.

Lacan, J. (1997) *The Seminar of Jacques Lacan: The Psychoses (Book III)* (J.-A. Miller, ed.; R. Grigg, translator). W. W. Norton & Company.

Lacan, J. (2018). *The Seminar of Jacques Lacan: The Four Fundamental Concepts of Psychoanalysis (Book XI)* (J.-A. Miller, ed.; A. Sheridan, translator). Routledge.

Lacan, J. (2021). *The Object Relation: The Seminar of Jacques Lacan, Book IV* (J.-A. Miller, ed.; A. R. Price, translator). Polity Press.

*Merriam-Webster Dictionary* (2020). G. & C. Merriam Co.

Nusbaum, M. (2018). *Monarchy of Fear*. Simon & Schuster.

Paarlberg, R. (2015). *The United States of Excess*. Oxford University Press.

Piketty, T. (2014). *Capital in the Twenty-First Century*. Harvard University Press.

Slosar, J. (2009). *The Culture of Excess. How America Lost Self-Control and Why We Need to Redefine Success*. Bloomsbury Publishing.

Spiner, T. (2022). Special report: 14 emerging trends. *American Psychological Association: Monitor, 53* (1), 42.

Twenge, J. M., & Donnelly, K. (2016). Generational differences in American students' reasons for going to college, 1971–2014: The rise of extrinsic motives. *The Journal of Social Psychology,* 156: 6, 620–629. https://doi.org/10.1080/00224 545.2016.1152214

# Chapter 6

# A Tipping Point?

At the conclusion of the *Wonder Woman* film of 2017, Wonder Woman comes to a powerful realization. She has defeated a world enemy, believing that victory would then free humanity from all the world's evil—bringing full human goodness to finally be restored. And yet, after all the excessive destructiveness she has overcome, she realizes that while she has always wanted to bring peace, harmony, and light to mankind, that both darkness and light are not simply outside and elsewhere, but that there is a bit of both living within every single human being. She realizes that, as such, each person must choose in their life how to act upon this darkness and light. No hero can overcome or save them from this dual reality, or from their own choice.[1]

Another way to see Wonder Woman's epiphany is that psychic light and darkness are both essential parts of the human condition, *and* that they dwell within both the conscious and unconscious parts of our minds—as well as in their interplay—in all of us. It is about time for the collective/social unconscious to takes its place at the table of a nation that claims its own exceptionalism and strives to lead in the world.

## Ripe Times for Change

It is a universal human experience that a "big something" or a "series of smaller somethings" can occur, causing us to become decentered, and bring us to the realization that our life is somehow different from how we once thought it is, or would be. These "somethings" can come from sources external to us, like an unexpected death or loss of a loved one; a terrible physical injury or a life-threatening diagnosis; a sudden job loss; or, on the plus side, the encountering of some new beloved person who tilts the axis of our world in a positive direction.

These "somethings" can also come from unconscious sources internal to us, causing our usual ways of coping to falter and/or our defenses to weaken. These kinds of breakthroughs make unconscious elements of ourselves more accessible to us, and bring us the opportunity to harvest unconscious material. When this occurs, it is a "ripe time for change."

DOI: 10.4324/9781032677309-7

These same occurrences also happen on a group and societal level, as is the case of our recent (and current) shared experience of a worldwide pandemic where societies have been de-centered and ruptured, and where people have felt existentially threatened. On a parallel track during these last several years, there have been an escalating series of climate-change disasters—bigger and stronger hurricanes, fires, floods, and tornados; the hottest years on record. We've witnessed more and more violence—school shootings, the January 6, 2021 insurrection, increased gun suicides, Putin's unlawful invasion of Ukraine—the largest European military assault since the Second World War. All of these events are yelling "Emergency!" "Emergency!" to our human psyches. And these de-centerings of excess are pushing America and the entire democratic world toward a re-organization of thinking. As cases in point, Finland and Sweden only now are joining NATO as the group of nations committed to democracy and its defense.

At an individual level, when a person cannot process psychic pain, that pain can fall back into the body and lodge there, where it can, and sometimes does lead to physical illness.[2] So too, at the group level, humanity's failure to process its own psychic pain adequately is now moving us toward the ongoing destruction of American democracy and that of other democratic countries—as well as a destruction of our shared body: planet Earth. With the fast-approaching tipping point of 1.5° Celsius (2.7° Fahrenheit), we are literally creating our own Dante's Inferno on Earth—a hell with disproportionate global effects. The increase in these climate disasters in tandem with the Covid pandemic, and the Ukrainian civilian atrocities wrought by Russia, are all helping bring home in a visceral manner that loss and death threaten all of us, not just certain disenfranchised "others."

Regardless of their point of origin, these breakthroughs of "excess" create painful periods of disorganization in the "usual" self or the "usual" group identity. These ruptures can be responded to as opportunities for change and psychic growth, or as "excessive disasters" generating an urgency to re-establish the "old order" as quickly as possible. (In the US we see such "old order" efforts in the Supreme Court's 2022 recent spate of decisions—banning abortion, banning affirmative action in college admissions, enabling the public carrying of guns, restricting government efforts to improve climate conditions.)

But on the growth side, there is the highly visible anecdotal example of the breakthrough of unconscious material learned from one's excesses by George W. Bush. During Bush's 2022 speech at his presidential library in Dallas, Texas, Bush railed against Putin's violent invasion of Ukraine. He condemned, "... the decision of one man to launch a wholly unjustified and brutal invasion of ..." What we expected to hear was "Ukraine." Instead, what Bush said out loud was "a wholly unjustified and brutal invasion of IRAQ." He then stumbled, correcting himself, "I mean Ukraine!" And then he admitted, "Well Iraq, too ..." His Freudian slip revealed a breakthrough of his unconscious knowledge—waiting to be claimed—and that he *did* claim—regarding his own excess in the violent "Shock and Awe" campaign against Iraq in 2003.[3]

In contrast, we have Trump's January 6, 2021 address on the Ellipse to his armed supporters, urging them to march to the Capitol and "fight like hell" —only to be followed by his very reluctant public statement (urged by many of his allies) hours into the attack, asking the mob to finally withdraw when they were not successful in overturning the electoral count. "I love you," he said. "You're very special ... Go home, and go home in peace." These were his words on the afternoon of January 6, 2021. But in the background of memory were also his words to white supremacists on September 29, 2020, to "Stand back and stand by." To date, there is no evidence of insight he has gleaned from the excesses he has fomented. The hanging question is this: Will time, as in the case of George Bush, open him to any awaiting unconscious knowledge? Not likely ...

### The Time Limits On Ripeness

A "ripe time" time for moving along into transformational change never lasts indefinitely. "Ripeness" for change and growth will be extinguished in time as the usual self or societal organization strives and struggles to regain control once again. We have a clear demonstration of this dynamic in the swell of the Black Lives Matter (BLM) protests during the pandemic, reflecting a broad white cultural shift in empathy and interest in American reparations to the descendants of slavery. It is of note that half of the 377 Confederate statues taken down across the country occurred during the pandemic after the murder of George Floyd. And yet 2,083 Confederate memorials still do remain—and—bans against the teaching of "critical race theory" in a number of states have followed the BLM swell.[4] This is just one example of how ripeness for change and growth always exists in tension with counter-maneuvers to deny and repress the reality of what an experience of excess can offer in terms of knowledge waiting for interpretation.

Within turbulent currents of excess (culminating in Trump as a symbolic and real phenomenon himself), we are standing at the precipice of events and movements that could portend a significant shift in cultural self-awareness. Can it be that the accumulating excesses of decades have been moving us forward in tipping-point fashion toward the possibility of a systemic change—where there is an awakening recognition that not only individuals, but groups and nations have, and do act upon unconscious processes? And that these processes must also be a part of human accountability. Were this movement toward awakening and recognition of unconscious influences to become fully realized in our societal thinking process, the social impact would be extensive!

The time for living an unexamined American life—in terms of both its unconscious and conscious factors—is over. Ripeness is a close cousin to "tipping point."[5] So in this ripening of times, there is a precariousness regarding transformational change. In today's polarized America, that change could tip in the direction of darkness or light in terms of feelings, values, thoughts, and behaviors. It is for this reason we see American excesses *foreshadowing* either *heralding or harbinger messages*—with *foreshadowing* becoming a new bead of meaning to be strung on the necklace that is called *excess*. The time of ripeness is tipping America into a crucible in which the outcome—positive (herald) or negative (harbinger)—is currently in process.

At the time of this chapter's writing, the 2022 mid-term election revealed "a heralding" message from excess—a tipping point toward light. Enough to verbal and violent extremism! Enough to omnipotent wishes and delusion! Or in other words, enough to "Trumpism's" perversion of truth in language and evocation of violence inherent in 2020 "election-deniers." Although approximately 150 election deniers were elected to the House, the number of House seats lost to the Republican party was the smallest loss from mid-term elections by any Democratic president of the last 40 years—despite predictions of a "red wave." As for the seats of power in governorships—positions that can impact elections greatly—it was the best result for Democrats since1986, particularly in those states Trump sought to overturn after his 2020 loss—by hook or by crook.[6] Thus overall, mid-term results were a rebuke by America's majority of Trump, Trumpism, and its tacit autocracy. Instead, the election was an affirmation of one person, one vote power and a profession of faith in and willingness to defend the workings of America's democracy. It was a positive message.

### And So, Within Our Ripening of Times: The Ever-Present Unconscious, Excess, and the Feminine

It has been broadly acknowledged that Hillary Clinton's loss was strongly influenced by unconscious sexism and misogyny, and it has been widely recognized by mental health experts and insightful others that many of Trump's thoughts and actions emanate from the unconscious realm of mind as attempts to deal with emotional injuries he is reported to have suffered in his family of origin. He has compensated for these injuries and deficits via multiple omnipotent identifications, including his identification as a masculine "tough guy"—a paragon of patriarchy—even though he escaped military service and has never proven himself on a field of battle. Nevertheless, he encourages identification with the "tough guy" persona. He stands upon and acts in excess without apology. He has assigned to himself the power to author and re-write truth—the 2020 election results being his most recent re-write. Fox News's Tucker Carlson, a pre-eminent advocate of "Trumpism," only furthered Trump's repetitive paranoid themes, veering farther and farther from material truth to inflame feelings of rejection, envy, hate, sexism, misogyny, and violence in his audience.[7] In this delusional context, is it possible that a powerful anvil of twenty-first-century feminism is being called to arms to destabilize and disassemble the platform that Donald Trump and "Trumpism" now stand on?

Part of women's exclusion from the highest levels of political and economic power has always been their relegation by the patriarchy to the task of tending to the newborn and very young of society—and, in that way, holding and marking the unconscious place in human functioning. (In other words, out of sight, out of mind.) Women do this routinely in their role as mothers—reading, making sense of, and responding to the non-verbal cues of infants; decoding the unspoken signals of children (and later, of intimate partners and, in the case of former House Speaker Nancy Pelosi, many colleagues!). Patriarchal societies overall diminish what women bring to the table as "less significant"—in part because of their association with that unconscious time in all our lives and that is beyond our memory. In this relegation, however, there is a "tell"—because many in the culture know there is a potent unconscious layer of the human mind, but act as if they don't know, or don't understand, its significance.

And finally, in the world of male privilege, women, since the time of Eve and her descendants, have also been psychically assigned the place of "excess" in society in four significant ways: (1) being less physically strong than men, so being unable to impose their will on others—so they can be excessed; (2) being concerned with the least powerful in the culture—society's children—so being of lesser value in the marketplace of goods and ideas; (3) being the repositories of all of the excess that falls outside of explicit, worded meanings—thus holding and representing such ineffable elements as intuition, empathy, beauty, and witchcraft's dark powers etc.; and (4) being assigned a subordinate place, and held in contempt for things perceived as threatening to the patriarchy, such as feminine power, female desire, ambition, sexuality, and assertive aggression. These are things that are defined as belonging only to men and/or make women less feminine. What a sleight of hand!

As suggested in prior chapters, personal and societal excess in all its different forms can crack open the possibility of *access* to useful, growth-promoting, unconscious knowledge—if approached with curiosity and openness. The patriarchy, however—with its elements of both sexism and misogyny—is staunchly defended by its membership. Why would it choose, after all, to lay down its power? It is in patriarchy that the strongest social resistance lives—resistance living within both genders across the world—to accepting and promoting feminine sensibilities and female leadership. Along with persistent racism, this is an element of American white women's presidential voting pattern. Within many societies, there is an unconscious "no" that has to be overcome for a woman to reach "executive power" and hold life and death power over its citizenry—once *again*—like all our mothers once did!

It is with all this in mind that we have come to imagine aspects of another kind of American feminism—a feminism specifically including an *additional register: active consideration of the unconscious influences within ourselves, as well as in others* It is our contention that the deepest level of psychic progress is achieved when something moves from the unconscious mind of possibility to the conscious mind's "assumption" that this something is, or should be, elemental to one's personal identity. Likewise, in national terms, the deepest level of psychic progress is achieved when one's national identification can also shift. A broader recognition of the reality of unconscious elements in human life, individually and nationally, would go beyond Andrew Yang's presidential slogan of "Make America Think Again"—to help America—for the first time—"Think Differently."

Moving in this direction then, we now go to Part 2 to consider today's generational levers of change, by first stepping back in Chapter 7—into history as a mythic foundation—to set both an emotional tone and context for the past and, hopefully, toward the future, going forward. This mythical presentation can serve as imaginative fuel for feminism's twenty-first-century "warrior work" of bringing in a different register. Therefore, we go now to the pre-Biblical creation story of Lilith and visit the scene of that very first "battle of the sexes"—in how it illustrates the very salient and potent notion of the "return of the repressed."

## Notes

1  Patty Jenkins's 2017 film *Wonder Woman*: "I used to want to save the world, to end war and bring peace to mankind—but then, I glimpsed the darkness that lives inside their lights and learned that within every one of them, there will always be both—a choice each must make for themselves—something no hero will ever defeat."
2  See Felitti et al. (1998) on adverse childhood experiences (ACEs) and subsequent research. See also, van der Kolk (2014).
3  In the vein of excess, the Twin Tower attacks of 9/11 were employed by the Bush administration to make an excessive response of invading Iraq (and already planned in Cheney's mind) and Afghanistan, rather than searching for and bringing Bin Laden to justice. This Bush excess resulted in years of excess—a 20-year-war—reminiscent to many boomers of the years-long tragedy of US troops in Vietnam.
4  Cataloged by the Southern Poverty Law Center's (2022) *The Year in Hate & Extremism Report 2021*.
5  Gladwell's first book *The Tipping Point* was published in 2002. Perhaps Bush's 9/11 response was a first in the US military path of excess in this century.
6  The governorship of Georgia—a state where Trump sought to overturn 2020 results—was won by a Republican in the 2022 mid-term election, but a Republican who did not endorse the "big lie."
7  See Confessore (2022) for an extensive researched piece on Tucker Carlson's evolution and the tabulation of the themes of "us versus them" in anti-immigration,

anti-feminism, elitism of the ruling class, racist tropes etc., with an increasing intensity through the Trump years—especially following his 2020 loss and the "big lie" conscription that followed.

## References

Confessore, N. (2022). What to know about Tucker Carlson's rise. *The New York Times*, April 30. https://www.nytimes.com/2022/04/30/business/media/tucker-carlson-fox-news-takeaways.html

Felitti, V. J., Anda, R. F., Nordenberg, D., et al. (1998). Relationship of childhood abuse and household dysfunction to many of the leading causes of death in adults. The Adverse Childhood Experiences (ACE) Study. *American Journal of Preventive Medicine*, *14*(4), 245–258. https://doi.org/10.1016/s0749-3797(98)00017-8

Jenkins, P. (2017). *Wonder Woman*. USA: Warner Bros./DC Comics. 2(9), 24–28.

Politico.com (2023). Election Results 2022: Live Map: Mid-term Races by State, politico.com, February 23. https://www.politico.com/2022-election/results/

van der Kolk, B. (2014). *The Body Keeps the Score*. Routledge.

# Part 2

## Changing the Narrative

# Chapter 7

# A Return of the Repressed
## Lilith Arising

Whenever and whatever part of us seeks to be known—by either provoca-
tion or eruption—it is a chance, an opportunity to re-member—to become
more of yourself.

We now want to take you on a mythical voyage, because myths, for centuries,
were our sciences and philosophies—our vehicles for explaining the how and
why of the world, and of ourselves. When we think about the current state
of our culture, and how much it has inclined itself in the direction of such
masculine pursuits as power, acquisitiveness, dominance, and conquest, we
look for ways to explain what there is and what is lacking. Often, the artistic
expressions of a culture reflect the culture, but are also constrained by the
culture itself. So, to get beyond the bounds of our current cultural ossifica-
tions, we looked beyond those sources, into an ancient mythical expression
of the potentials of the feminine, and what it may offer to us in this time of
upheaval and cultural uncertainty.

## Lilith and Adam, and the First Battle of the Sexes

There is much to consider in a short Babylonian creation myth about the first
woman—the story of Lilith.[1] This myth preceded the creation story of Adam
and Eve portrayed in the Book of Genesis. Just as America's political crossing into the twenty-first century was marked by "hanging chads" that the
Supreme Court ruled would not be counted,[2] the Lilith origin story suggests
multiple "hanging chads" concerning human dignity and justice in diverse
realms.[3] This creation myth points to gender and sexuality themes that, in
many ways, have been discounted, not counted, or counted out in American
life and culture, and may, in fact help us to chart a different course as we go
forward.

DOI: 10.4324/9781032677309-9

The myth goes like this:

Long, long ago and far, far away ...

*Lilith was the first woman, created by God from the matter of earth, like Adam, the first man—both made from the same soil. Soon Lilith and Adam began to argue over who should "lie beneath" the other during sex. Lilith soon became aware that Adam wanted her to play a subservient role and that neither was listening to the other, so she uttered the name of God and "flew into the air of the word," running away to reside by the sea. Adam complained to God that Lilith had run away. God then sent three angels, Senoi, Sansenoi, and Sammangelof to retrieve her. The three angels found Lilith in a cave, bearing children, but Lilith refused to come back to the garden. The angels told her they would kill 100 of her children every day for her disobedience. She still refused, and the angels could not make her return. Later elaborations of the story told of her returns from the Red Sea at night to visit men in their sleep, bringing them wet dreams.*

This first creation story was altered and rewritten over time. Of the *two mythical versions of the creation story, ultimately, only the second version—* that of Eve and Adam—remained in the Bible's Book of Genesis.

Today the mythical figure of Lilith offers us a potent symbol of a psychological process known as the "return of the repressed." As discussed in Chapter 2, this process refers to something below the conscious mind (banned from the conscious layer of the mind and pushed into the unconscious), but which pushes for a return to the conscious mind—in a reach for recognition and further psychic integration. As we move forward into the chapters ahead, we invoke Lilith as a necessary symbol of the "return of the repressed." We see in the Lilith myth a possible model for the integration of the missing or diminished elements of the feminine in current American culture. We turn to Lilith for her influence over the psychic health of women, yes, but for that of the entire culture as well.

So, in the Lilith origin story then, what are those hanging chads?

1  Loss of gender equality in material standing.

In this original myth, woman and man are created out of the same material: Earth's soil. Male and female start out equal. A remnant of this gender equality is contained in the *first* Biblical creation account in Genesis 1, in the phrase: "in the image of God he created them; male and female he created them."[4] But it is the Bible's *second* creation story of Adam and Eve in Genesis 2 where Eve is made entirely differently—not from equal substance, but from Adam's rib.[5] Therefore, Eve begins life as "one down" and with less than equal footing to walk into her future. Worse yet, Eve, when she does take a walk on her own, will become culturally linked to "sin" and "excess" from her very first encounter.

2  Woman's loss of authority to speak.

Looking at the power of language within the original creation story, Lilith spoke the name of God in the very moment she left the scene of this *first "battle of the sexes"*—"flying into the air of the word." Lilith's speaking God's name (an act which was then, and for a long time since, forbidden) can be interpreted as her seizing power over her own destiny. God accepted this power of language, recognizing the validity of her claim for individual subjectivity via her refusal of the angels' call for her to return to Adam. God did not *force her return*—instead he set consequences for her choice and a different framework of both the limits and degrees of freedom to her life.

Further evidence of this inherent power of language may be seen in the fact that the names of the three angels were sufficient to protect the infants whom Lilith was told she was destined to threaten. Also, in later mythical stories about Lilith, in her surreptitious returns from the Red Sea, she would promise to forsake her threatening ways, if that threatened person would call her by one, or all, of her fourteen names. In this we see the very human need to be named and recognized in words. To name is to empower and authorize a legitimate "self"—one's own unique self, or the separate and unique self of another.[6]

The power invested in language—the words to say "yes" or "no" to entering any agreement is missing in the Biblical story of Eve and Adam. There is talk between Eve and the serpent, and talk between Eve and God, but there is no mention of any verbal exchange between Eve and Adam. There are exchanges between Adam and God during which Adam lays the first gendered blame for *his eating* of the apple on Eve.

3  Loss of female legitimate personal agency and curiosity.

Lilith enters the discussion with Adam, argues for justice, decides to emotionally withdraw, and finally physically leaves when a verbal impasse is reached. In contrast, Eve's single, but profound, expression of independent energy and agency—eating the forbidden fruit—has catastrophic consequences, causing the couple's expulsion from the Garden of Eden, and consigning Eve and all women to a future of painful childbirth.

Biblical history dismisses the value of Eve's curiosity and thirst for knowledge. It emphasizes instead Eve's disobedience to God in her wanting more than what is offered in the Garden of Eden. Excessive! It also condemns her emotional excess in seducing Adam to join her in eating the apple. (Notably, her initiative to include Adam as an equal partner in her adventure is maligned.) Thus, what is seen as her exercise of "excess" condemns her with a forever mark of "original sin"—not only her, but a mark to be left on all mankind.[7]

4  Loss of female sexual desire and access to sexual pleasure.

Sexuality is a critical playing field within the story of Lilith and Adam. In fact, sensual play is an operative element that is lost in the sexual power struggle when Adam refuses to be "a bottom." A verbal negotiation does begin, but turns conflictual, and when talk comes to an impasse, Lilith takes her freedom and flees—her flight empowered by speaking the name of God! Although Lilith's sexuality and fertility are freighted with loss by the sheer number of children who must be sacrificed as penance for her refusal of the angels' command, female sexuality is at least still registered and marked as potent. (Later elaborations of the Lilith story also mention her seeking sexual enjoyment through her surreptitious returns to men in the night.) In the creation story of Eve, however, there is a complete absence of the pleasure of human sexuality—female or male. Sex is referenced only by its utilitarian function—reproduction—and linked to punishment and pain for Eve's having expressed a "desire for more" in response to tantalizing temptation by another.

5  Loss of female physical reproductive and creative autonomy.

A related aspect to the hanging chad of sexuality is the mention of Lilith's having 100 children a day. Such a clearly mythical/surreal notion raises a question about female creativity and biological reproduction. How has the biological capacity for bearing children been used to foreclose or invalidate women's other creative potentials? The sheer number of children Lilith bears proffers the possibility of imagining different kinds of creative productions from women (other than biological children). The myth of Lilith also opens an imaginal space between being biologically female and inhabiting a psychic feminine position (this is explored in Chapter 11).

In the final chapter of the 1993 book, *Reconceiving Women: Separating Motherhood from Female Identity*, the creation story of Lilith was used as a metaphor for the energies that reside, or could reside, in women who do not become mothers—to facilitate their taking up their full place in society. For women who are mothers, these energies may remain unexpressed because they can lean primarily into their identity as mothers. To be female, in essence, means to bear children. This is the main route to social recognition for women. We've come some distance in the last 30 years in making room for Lilith-inspired energies. As one woman cited in the above book observed, "the term 'old maid' is no longer being used to talk about single women."[8] But, we are still working out the choices open to and foreclosed from women.

6  Loss of both gender and racial equality.

Very *present* by its *absence*—there is no reference to skin color in the cre-ation stories of either Lilith or Eve. In both stories, what is at stake is the essential creation of human beings as distinct from other living creatures on earth. Skin color is a non-essential. From current times we may wonder how centuries later, in the earliest recorded painting of Eve and Adam, the pair are portrayed by Albrecht Dürer (1507) as distinctly white, even though the cradle of humanity was very likely to have been Northern Africa.[9] Thus, a Western fantasy of the origins of mankind, imagined as foundational a few centuries ago, was established. It has been defended since then, and has been fought for by its beneficiaries in order to relegate social/political power to one privileged group of human beings—white men.[10]

## In Closing, An Opening

The myth of Lilith promotes avenues of strength, creativity, and self-determination for women. It was in thinking about Lilith versus Eve after the 2016 election that we began to imaginatively wonder: were Lilith not "commanded" by angels to a return that would make her less than a man—if she were instead, "respectfully entreated" by the angels, would the spirit of Lilith have returned, helping women to reclaim even more of the parts of themselves that had been abrogated in the Book of Genesis? How would it have looked for Lilith to return on her own terms—not to take a subservient position to a man as was expected—nor to sneak back from time to time in the dark of night to fulfill sexual and other desires—but just to return as an equal human being in broad daylight?

So, in this spirit, we metaphorically began to call upon Lilith as our archetype of the potentials of the feminine—to take a more crucial role in shaping feminism for this century. Surely twenty-first-century feminism needs her spirit and her energies! Perhaps we've even begun to see her impact. In the 2018 American election cycle, the highest number ever of American female, racially diverse, and LGBTQ individuals were elected to local, state, and national office![11] On a lighter, but telling note, within the popular world of Marvel Cinematic Universe, we saw a shift begin in 2018—in their release of *Black Panther*—shifting from exclusively fea-turing white male heroes, to include women and/or persons of color as central to their films.

In this century there is a call to further de-repress the females roots of empowerment represented in the Lilith myth—to fully unleash the power, creativity, sexuality, and multiplicity of desire inherent in the heritage of women. It has never been more needed than now with the repeal of female bodily autonomy in the 2022 Dobbs' ruling! Fifty years of female bodily integrity and freedom of choice erased—wiped out by six people in the face of a vast majority of Americans thinking otherwise![12] In this regard, all feminists, of all genders, would do well to draw from all that Lilith represents!

We turn now to the levers of change, focused on who, what, and where Lilith-infused warrior work could be focused. The next chapter describes elements of the last fifty years of the boomer generation as a scaffold for the challenges faced by millennials if they are to take up the warrior work of overcoming unconscious, as well as conscious, forces inhibiting full gender equality and human justice. Millennials are specifically highlighted here because they have now displaced boomers as the *largest generation*, and as such, they now have their opportunity—their turn—for making a substantial impact on the evolution of American culture.

## Notes

1  See Ben-Amos (2016).
2  In regard to the SCOTUS 2000 ruling on "hanging chads"—successful efforts over decades by Republicans to establish right-leaning court justices, up to, and including, the Supreme Court, have been framed by some as elemental to the Bush campaign's successful challenge brought to the Florida vote count to stop the counting of the "hanging chads." This challenge resulted in the Supreme Court delivering the electoral win to Bush. (This court decision was in keeping with the conservative Republicans ongoing strategy of suppressing the vote—seemingly because when such measures did not occur—the Democrats won.). See also Sunstein and Epstein (2001).
   Did the insertion of this court decision into an election embolden Bush's impulsive/excessive rush to war after 9/11? Whether it was or not, this decision was an early twenty-first-century mark of excess by the sheer absence of thinking about what part, that Bush labeled as "hate" toward America, was in fact our own.
3  Discovered later in Griffith (2022), Elizabeth Cady Stanton was accused of heresy and censured for citing the creation version of Adam and Eve as being made of equal material in her book *The Woman's Bible* in 1845.
4  See Zondervan's *Quest Study Bible* (Revised) (2003) for an annotated approach to Biblical reading.
5  Again, Zondervan's *Quest Study Bible* (Revised) (2003) for an annotated approach to Biblical reading.
6  It is no accident the frequency with which women often spell their names in unique ways, take on special nicknames of their own, or in recent times, take on a man's last name in marriage by addition by using a hyphen rather than ablating their own surname—all show the significance of personal instantiation through language.
7  The Augustinian Theory. This is also called the Theory of Adam's Natural Headship and the Realistic Theory—see Gulley (1994). This theory was formulated by Augustine in the fifth century CE. The Augustinian Theory affirms that, by virtue of organic unity, the whole human race existed in Adam at the time of his transgression. It says that Adam's will was the will of the species, so that in Adam's free act, the will of the race revolted against God, and the nature of the race corrupted itself. All men existed as one moral person in Adam, so that in Adam's sin

we sinned, we corrupted ourselves, and we brought guilt and merited condemnation upon ourselves. It is hard not to read this as both politically and patriarchally motivated propaganda for Christianity in a world of competing world religions.

8  See Ireland (1993).

9  See Albrecht Dürer's (1507) painting *Adam and Eve* (two panels), Museo del Prado, Madrid, Spain. Also, Ragsdale et al. (2023).

10  Worth a reminder: white men colonized more than people and governments, but also language, i.e., books initially were only available to a select few—primarily white men of the Church.

11  See Houck (2018) for demographics of elected officials in the 2018 election.

12  Hartig (2022) indicates that 60% of Americans want legal abortion to be available nationally.

## References

Ben-Amos, D. (2016). From Eden to Ednah—Lilith in the Garden. *Biblical Archaeology Review*, 42(3), 54–58. https://repository.upenn.edu/nelc_papers/142.

Dürer, A. (1507). *Adam and Eve (two panels)*, Museo del Prado, Madrid, Spain. https://www.wikiart.org/en/albrecht-durer/adam-and-eve-1507#:~:text=Adam%20and%20Eve%20is%20a,depict%20the%20ideal%20human%20figure

Griffith, E. (2022). *Formidable: American Women and the Fight For Equality: 1920–2020*. Pegasus.

Gulley, N. (1994). The effects of Adam's sin on the human race. *Journal of the Adventist Theological Society*, 5(1), art. 9. https://digitalcommons.andrews.edu/jats/vol5/iss1/9/

Hartig, H. (2022). About six-in-ten Americans say abortion should be legal in all or most cases. Pew Research Center, June 13. https://www.pewresearch.org/short-reads/2022/06/13/about-six-in-ten-americans-say-abortion-should-be-legal-in-all-or-most-cases-2/

Houck, C. (2018). Muslim women, Native Americans, and LGBTQ candidates had a night of historic wins. *Vox*, November 7. www.vox.com/2018/11/7/18072658/midterm-election-results-historic-wins-muslim-native-american-women.

Ireland, M. (1993) *Reconceiving Women: Separating Motherhood From Female Identity*. Guilford Press.

*Quest Study Bible*, Revised (2003). Zondervan Corporation.

Ragsdale, A. P., Weaver, T. D., Atkinson, E. G. et al. (2023). A weakly structured stem for human origins in Africa. *Nature*, 617, 755–763. https://doi.org/10.1038/s41586-023-06055-y

Sunstein, C. & Epstein, R. (2001). *The Vote: Bush, Gore, and the Supreme Court*. University of Chicago.

# Chapter 8

# Moving Forward

## 20th-Century Boomers to 21st-Century Millennials

"Every generation blames the one before.
And all their frustrations come beating on your door ...
We all talk a different language—talking in defense"[1]
*The Living Years*

We turn now to look at the two largest generations of Americans—the boomers and the millennials—keeping in mind the idea that both conscious and unconscious elements are transmitted across generations. Boomers were the post-Second World War generation (born 1946–1964), followed by Gen X (born 1965–1980), millennials (born 1981–1996), Gen Z (born 1997–2012), and Gen Alpha (born 2013–2025). The apex year in size and political participation of the baby boom generation was 1999; the millennials came of age and surpassed the boomers in size and political participation in 2016.

To look back 50 years (2024–1974) is to understand something about what the present generations have assumed as "a given." It is also to understand that some of those assumptions are a result of things consciously worked toward in the prior 50 years—with the hope that the gains achieved would make it across the generations—by being actively learned, or sometimes, by just becoming integrated into the collective unconscious. Either way, such transmission has, at least in part, happened.

The baby boomers and then the millennials are the two current generations that, due to their size, have wielded—or will wield—disproportionate impact on society throughout their lifespans.

Boomers' births started in 1946, coincident with the end of the Second World War. Their political influence would thus have begun to be evident as the first boomers reached college age in 1964. (As a historical note, in July 1964, 5000 additional US military advisers were ordered to South Vietnam, bringing the total American troop level to 21,000. The cumulative American death toll in 1964 was 416. Six years later, in 1970, the cumulative death toll was 54,909. Major losses began to attenuate until 1973, when the US pulled

DOI: 10.4324/9781032677309-10

out of Vietnam. By the end of the conflict, the death toll—largely boomers—was 58,220.)[2]

Boomers became the largest segment of the workforce in 1999 (when the first boomers were 53 and last boomers were 35). Accordingly, they became the most economically dominant segment of the population in 1999, coincident with the shift into the twenty-first century.

Seventeen years later, in 2016, millennials passed the baby boomers in their sheer numbers, and therefore, in their potential generational impact. Because the size of generations has a disproportionate impact on a culture, we highlight in this chapter aspects of each generation's experiences, aims and effects, finally focusing in on the worlds of boomer and millennial women.

## Zooming Out—A 50-Year Lens: Boomers To Millennials

### The Boomers—A Generation of Excess

The baby boomers—the largest generation extant—could be said to have been bred from what Mae West called "the good kind of excess"—that of desire and hope, following the Allied victory in the Second World War. Perhaps in the atmospherics of post-Second World War expansiveness—spawned by the forces of light triumphing over the forces of darkness—a sector of the boomer generation pushed for more light to triumph in multiple human arenas—race, gender, sexual orientation, social economics—during the 1960s and early 1970s. A large segment of this generation protested the Vietnam War, seeing it as an expression of patriarchal colonization, and as a meaningless war which was depleting their generation. They also acted against policies of despoiling Planet Earth for capitalistic gains.

When birth control access (1960)[3] and abortion became legal (1973), boomers initiated a sexual revolution, even exploring "open relationships" (with rather mixed longer-term results).[4] For the first time in America, women's bodies became their own province, and their life choices widened—something that Gen X and millennials would come to take for granted (until June 2022, when they couldn't anymore). Boomers also experimented with mind-altering drugs and alcohol significantly more than the generation before them or generations to follow.[5]

Boomers pursued self-actualization in many forms. Drugs, sex, and rock & roll captured a large segment of boomers.[6] Among activist boomers, a distrust of established institutions was seeded, and the revelations in the Pentagon Papers confirmed their shared suspicions. A contingent of them expressed this in various forms of "dropping out" and countercultural pursuits.[7] Activist boomers experienced their social idealism under direct attack from government sources. They suffered the shock wave of the Kent State police shootings of unarmed students (1970), killing four and wounding nine,[8] and witnessed the assassinations of several of their treasured political and activist leaders.

A large percentage of boomers, however, still saw the world they came into as promising them a good life—if only they worked hard and followed the societal rules and expectations of a post-war America. Of course, these opportunities were racially segmented, and the professional horizon for boomer women was quite limited (despite their working mothers' contribution to the Second World War)

A plethora of scholars and essayists have focused on understanding the cultural impact of the 1960s, as well as a certain puzzling turn from lightness to darkness in the boomers.[9] This profile draws on these sources, as well as on our own lived experience as two white, female boomers. If boomers were born of a kind of positive excess, they also turned toward problematic and destructive excess as well.

Even with an initial general optimism for the future, the very size of this generation made for circumstances of intense competition among them for resources—i.e., educational, social, and employment opportunities. So, compete they did! But with such fierce competition that there were significant downsides.

Boomers' historical circumstance as a large, competitive cohort contributed to creating in them, as parents, a phenomenon that would come to be known as "helicopter parenting"—boomer parents striving to make sure that *nothing* would be lacking for their own children in making them competitive for the world's goods and rewards. One consequence of this helicoptering has been the decades of over-emphasis on the importance of getting high grades in order to succeed, of getting their children into the "right" schools, of pushing their children into multiple structured extra-curricular activities, and of positioning them to get that first "right" job, etc.

Concomitantly, this trend also brought a diminution of familial and cultural attention to the development of certain character attributes in boomers' children. Cultivation of such important values as honesty, nurturance, empathy, trustworthiness, group consciousness—in familial, business, social, and political relationships—began to attenuate. This trend led to the slow depletion of the kind of individual and group empathy required to mitigate the forces of aggression and destructiveness that are inherent to a purely narcissistic and materialistic pursuit of success. For example, a study tracking boomers' children—college students from 1982 to 2006—showed a 30% increase in narcissism.[10]

With respect to boomers themselves, as the excess of social idealism among a segment of the boomer generation began to be eroded over time by the larger group's seeking to succeed in the marketplace, there arose a concomitant re-orientation toward more material success. The interpretation of what the "American Dream" had meant thus began to change for boomers. Home ownership, entry into the middle class, and a satisfying family life as an American Dream morphed more and more into material success as a pre-eminent goal. "Success as excess" would become the way of a large swath of the boomer generation. The significant increase in enrollment in MBA programs since 1994, as well as the elimination of academic departments that did not translate into immediate high-paying employment, reflect this cultural shift.[11]

For many boomers, the pursuit of success took over where the generation's idealism left off. More and more of what success came to mean in the Boomer generation was less about social change, and more about the accumulation of wealth—not just enough money, but money in excess amounts. Between 1979 and 2007, the average income of the top 1% of boomers grew by 200%,[12] while the average income of the remaining 99% of US taxpayers grew by just 18.9%. Indeed, the top 1% in America took home well over half (53.9%) of the total increase in US income. Simultaneously, boomer computer/tech launchers—followed by the many IT start-ups in Silicon Valley—only enhanced this pursuit of excessive wealth.[13] As a direct or indirect result, America currently experiences more financial inequity than any other industrialized democracy.[14]

It is now well known that economic inequality has become much, much greater since the time when those young boomers were fretting about getting into college and obtaining those first jobs. The boomer generation is the wealthiest generation in American history. The rhetoric of the 1%-ers versus the 99%-ers has fomented a major sense of discontentment among many today, and a significant element of the boomer generation has directly participated in creating those inequities.[15] According to a May 16, 2023 *New York Times* article on transfer of wealth across generations, half of America's wealth is held by boomers. Most of the wealth transfer will then be coming in the next ten years. It will be only the top 10% of the wealthiest households who will be making most of this transfer. The bottom 50% of households will only be transferring 8% of that wealth.

Economic disparity is not solely an American phenomenon, of course.[16] Financial disparity is increasing globally as well. Yet, given that the US is the most influential and richest country in the world, it is unthinkable that in 2022 approximately 14% of the American population still lived in poverty. This is particularly sobering, given that it has been 50 years since the "War on Poverty" was declared by Lyndon Johnson (1964). In that time, the disparity between rich and poor has only increased.[17]

The first boomers (born in 1946) turned 25 in 1971. They turned 35 in 1981. One view of the 1980s is that a large segment of the boomer generation joined with conservative champion Ronald Reagan in a counter-reaction to the civil rights and social equity gains which had been achieved during the 1960s and 1970s. In the 1980s, when boomers were the dominant adult generation, there was a marked resurgence of religious fundamentalism, wherein the implicit social agenda became about turning back feminist gains and liberal social values. In the 1980s, Reaganomics ("supply-side economics"—slashing both taxes and social services, 1982–89) purposefully dismantled the safety net for social and mental health infrastructures, and set up a tax structure which supported spiraling financial inequities.

From the boomer's entry into a historical time of imagining they would move beyond their parents, they handed the next largest millennial generation a kind of capitalism-on-steroids[18]—with high stakes odds: astronomical success for some, but a dwindling future for most, as wages failed to keep up with productivity. Americans' wages have stagnated since the 1970s, with worker productivity *growing three times more than pay.*[19] Millennials would come to wonder if they could even reach parity with their own parents.

Boomer corporations "cooking the books" in the 1990s, as it became known, was a form of "cheating" to succeed—hiding greed and a lack of personal and institutional integrity under the cloak of success. Robert Hare, a leading expert on psychopathic behavior, suggested that American corporations, as they have evolved over the last three to four decades, are themselves psychopathic. Hasn't something been turned around here?, he asks. Why should it be that "what is good for business is good for the American people, instead of "what is good for the people is good for business.[20] Boomer, Donald Trump, elected president in 2016, personified this "unethical ethic," eschewing the ethical influences of relatedness and empathy.

Oscar Wilde once observed that, "Nothing succeeds like excess." This was certainly true during the boomer high time of 1980s and into the 1990s ... but mostly if you were male, well-educated, white, and straight. These categories bought membership in an ascendant, but increasingly exclusive financial class that transitioned from millionaires to billionaires over those decades.

On balance, the boomer generation will leave a mixed legacy—perhaps the lingering traces of the liberal and idealistic portion of the boomer generation who protested for systemic social change and environment-preserving policies. But perhaps boomers' more deeply etched and pernicious legacy will be their having helped to create a precarious economic structure for the next largest generation—the millennials.[21]

### The Millennials: A Generation of Hope

> "Maybe a great magnet pulls all souls towards truth,
> or maybe, it is life itself that gives wisdom to its youth ..."
> *Constant Craving*[22]

The competitive pressure to succeed and stand out from the horde of the large boomer generation fell forward onto its Gen X and millennial offspring.

An unfortunate consequence of boomers' perhaps well-intentioned over-attentiveness (and in some cases outright over-gratification) of their children was the creation in the millennial generation of a certain narcissistic expect-ation that everything for them would go as planned; that their "wish" would be someone else's "command." The push for success from their boomer parents may, in many cases, have come at the expense of building such char-acter resources as inner strength, integrity, and resilience. Observers have described many millennials as "entitled."[23] More children in the millen-nial generation have exhibited difficulty regulating self-esteem in the face of failure or loss.[24] Today's ubiquitous and persistent appearance of the selfie on social media—"I am here, I am here, and I am here now—look at me!"—is perhaps emblematic of their needing more *recognition from out-side* rather than having the *resources inside* themselves to regulate their fluc-tuating self-esteem.

Millennials from lower classes, where support provided by family and other social services has been attenuated since the 1980s, have been, in con-trast, left too much to raise themselves, as parents had to work multiple jobs because minimum wages never were living wages.[25] This reality has left them skeptical about the world of work generally—and perhaps about their own perceived value.

The pressure to succeed that millennials (born between1981–1996, begin-ning to enter college in 1999) internalized from boomer parents appears to have led not only to increased cheating in school, but also a comfort with doing so! A 2004 study reported that 62% of kids admitted to cheating—with the highest level of cheating occurring in privately funded religious schools![26] And although acknowledging the dishonesty of "cheating," the kids in the 2004 study reported that they were "ok" with their own personal ethics and character.[27] Cheating is likely to be even higher now. In fact, some millennial *parents* have been caught "cheating" by falsifying their kids' activ-ities and SAT scores to increase college admission chances.

We can say there is now a dueling national reality, wherein on the one hand, Americans think of themselves as honest and law-abiding—citizens of a democratic and compassionate nation—and on the other, Americans have developed a social norm that sees cheating as sometimes ok when it brings success of various kinds—from college admissions, to business, to elections—even to our presidential elections. Millennials have been left to struggle with this paradox.

For millennials, the legacy of their "over-involved" boomer parents has seeded additional negative effects—among them, a distrust of others and a tendency toward a transactional stance, a "default position" of challenging authority and inflating the value of their own credentials, opinions and ideas. These elements exist hand-in-glove with a deep longing for intimacy.[28]

So where has this left millennials in the financial marketplace? Almost *half of millennial renters* today think they will never be able to own a home, largely because of their inability to afford a down payment.[29] The cultural press for "success as excess" was the water they swam in, so the push for college has brought with it huge millennial debt. The cost of college tuition, fees, room, and board has more than doubled since the 1971–72 school years of boomers, adjusting for inflation. These climbing costs have burdened millions with student debt they struggle to pay off after graduating from college.[30]

So, the millennials, coming of age beginning in 1999, and entering the job market in their twenties, were jolted and decentered by the 9/11/2001 attack. Where was their place in an America under attack? Not long after that, they encountered the economic recession of 2008. The security of pensions from long-term employment of pre-boomer years had shifted over to 401K plans in 1978, when Congress passed the Revenue Act of 1978. The Act made long-term employment far less incentivized because pensions were replaced by 401K plans. Millennials moved (or were pushed) more toward a gig economy with resultant employment instability and difficulty to save for either property ownership and/or retirement.

A 50-year fly-over shows that the percentage of young adults who live in a parent's home more than doubled between 1971 and 2021—8% in 1971; 17% in 2021. Adjusted for inflation, millennials have one half as much wealth in their thirties as their boomer predecessors.[31] Also, in the fast-moving world of technology and in these times of excess, mid-life crises appear to be arriving earlier for millennials—bringing existential questions earlier and significant re-assessment of work and home during and after the pandemic years.

When, in 2015 (becoming the dominant generation in 2016), millennials became the largest segment of the workforce, they began to be able to flex their influence and push against the negatives that had been attached to them. They wanted meaningful work *and* connections at work. They wanted more personal accommodations and work flexibility. They wanted mental health coverage and they felt more comfortable pursuing psychotherapy than prior generations They wanted more work/life balance, as some began to turn away from the ethos of working in overdrive, pursuing the fantasized rewards of money in excess. Additionally, the values of the companies they worked for really mattered to them.

Millennials will likely be the biggest positive force in helping hybrid work situations endure—because home and personal relationships, work flexibility, business values, and even the meaning of personal freedom itself, is changing for millennials. In this change they are setting up different work environments and expectations for themselves (and for the upcoming Gen Z). Many millennials aim for earning enough for early retirement versus earning money in excess. This trend underlines how the American Dream may once again be re-etched in this generation.

Millennials are, in addition, the first truly digital generation. The online world became for them more and more a liminal space where millennials' lives are lived, launched ... and sometimes lost. Today millennials (and their kids) of every economic class have a smartphone—no longer just a phone. The Covid pandemic magnified this phenomenon for them—and for everyone— when in-person contact became dangerous to one's physical health. As a result, millennials and younger generations have all missed out on some important IRL (in real life) experiences—pushing them even more into a digital world. Meanwhile, the metaverse is taking a significant step forward, with virtual reality and AI heating up as the Covid pandemic has cooled for many in the millennial generation.[32] How virtual reality will intersect with the dynamics of seeking, and being in, real-life relationships for millennials is still early in its development. They are the first big *generation* having to wrestle with the impact of on-screen versus in-person relationships—and with what their differing standards of behaviors and meanings portend.

Millennials are also the first generation to have grown up with school shootings as a norm of their educational experience.[33] Boomers had drills for a nuclear attack; millennials had "active shooter" drills. Only in America. In 2021, the number of school shootings was higher (34) than any year since 1999's Columbine high school shooting.[34] Pew Research Center reports between 2019–2021, deaths of children by guns rose 50%—with gun deaths for black children being five times higher! America now has more instances of gun violence than any other country in the world. Millennials have inherited an excessive emphasis on America's value of *"individual freedom"* at the expense of the value of relatedness and social empathy. This imbalance, as noted in prior chapters, has been true in multiple venues, but none more visible and damaging than the issue of maintaining gun ownership of all types—at all costs. A *New York Times* investigative report from June 2022 noted that four laws—raising the minimum age to purchase certain guns; having legal consequences for those who fail to secure guns from children and criminals; expanding red-flag laws to remove guns from persons in crisis; and banning assault weapons—could have affected a third of the US mass shootings since 1999 that accounted for the deaths of 446 people.

Finally, a huge issue for everyone, but one that especially animates the millennials, is climate policy. In the 1980s, there were abundant early signs of global warming and climate problems, yet the threats to Mother Earth's existence were purposefully sidelined in the service of economic development. In the last 50 years, two-thirds of mammals, fish, reptiles, and amphibians species have been lost.[35] Rightly, millennials have asked, will there even be a viable planet for them and their children? Millennials in fact are having more one-child families than prior generations. They see the climate disasters coming; they also see the persistent lack of infrastructure supporting workers and their families that the Biden administration was attempting to address significantly in the Build Back Better legislation. The watered-down version of this Act, the Inflation Reduction Act, did include significant movement forward on climate policy. It should not be surprising there has been a pervasive sense of anxiety within this generation about their futures. Millennials' legitimate anger, plus their brand of demand-politics, will likely fuel more effective environmental policies in caring for "Mother Earth" in the future.

### Female Boomers to Female Millennials

We are constantly creating the world we inhabit. And what we sow today, another generation may indeed reap or be saddled with. So, having touched on aspects of both "largest" generations, we now turn to highlight the experience of women in these two generations, separated by 50 years, tracing especially the progress that has been made, and what may be at arms-reach to the millennial generation.

Today's millennials commonly eschew the "feminist" label per se but are the beneficiaries of strong "warrior work" by feminist boomers before them. Significant psychic progress is evident in today's millennials, who in fact simply *assume* their own gender equality and expect others to respect it—to a degree more than neither boomers nor Gen Xers were able to achieve. This progress was implicitly evident in the brave testimony of the two cusp millennials, Cassidy Hutchinson and Sarah Mathews, at the January 6, 2021 hearings.

What has changed in the 50 years separating the boomer and millennial generations? Let's look together at what emerging boomer females could anticipate as their "place" in the culture, and the limits on their life's horizons[36] in 1971.

### In 1971

The first female boomers (born 1946–1964) turned age 25 in 1971, at which time ...

- Women could not yet get a <u>credit card</u> in their own name (law passed 1974).
- Women were not legally permitted to obtain a mortgage without a male co-signer (law passed 1974).
- No legal action was available against workplace sexual harassment (until 1977).
- Working women could still be <u>fired for pregnancy</u> (pregnancy anti-discrimination law passed 1978).
- Abortion was illegal (access to legal birth control came in 1965 but legal access abortion not till 1973).

- Women could only serve in the military as nurses or support staff. (Only after 1973 could women serve in the military in roles other than nurses or support staff.)
- Sports funding in educational institutions was legally discriminatory. (Title IX, the non-discrimination law regarding sports funding in education, passed in 1972—a bit late for some aspiring female athletes of the boomer generation.)
- 74% of the best-selling books were by male authors; 26% by women. (The first woman publisher/CEO (Katherine Graham of *The Washington Post*) ascended to her position in 1972.)

### In 2006

As a comparison, let's also look at what feminist legacies the millennials were born into, and what remaining feminist challenges they face now and in the future. By 2006, adult female millennials (born 1981–1996; the firstborns of the millennials coming to age 25 in 2006), at which time …

- Could be financially separate and independent from male partners—credit cards, bank accounts, mortgages etc.
- Were legally protected from workplace sexual harassment.
- Could no longer be fired for pregnancy.
- Could obtain legal abortions.
- Could do many more jobs in the military if they chose.
- Were now recognized in professional sports, but were still striving for equal pay.
- Wrote 47% of the best-selling books; 53% were by male authors.[37]

*Table 8.1* A comparison in politics and business between female boomers and millennials at age 24 and 25

| The political/business world and potential of women in 1971 versus 2005 | First boomers 1971, age 25 | First millennials 2005, age 24 |
|---|---|---|
| Females in the US Senate | 1 | 14 |
| Females in the US House of Representatives | 13 | 60 |
| Female state governors | 0 | 8 |
| Female CEOs of Fortune 500 companies | 0 | 9 |
| Female network news anchors | 0 | dozens |
| Percentage of female vs male MDs | 8% | 47% |
| Percentage of female vs male attorneys | 6% | 29% |
| Percentage of female vs male college graduates | 43% | 56% |
| Percentage of female business managers | 16% | 42% |
| Earning power versus males performing equivalent jobs | 60¢/dollar | 81¢/dollar |

*Table 8.2* Social/educational/economic status of women, 1970–2020[38]

| Social/educational/economic status of women, 1970–2020 | First boomers (b. 1946) in 1970 | First millennials (b. 1981) in 2020 |
|---|---|---|
| % of women aged 25–34: Married | 81% | 43% |
| % of women aged 25–34: No children | 21% | 52% |
| % of women aged 25–44: College degree | 11% | 41% |
| % of women aged 15–44: No paying job | 55% | 27% |
| % of women aged 16–44: Jobs in management | 17% | 37% |
| % of women in heterosexual households where both partners worked where women's income > men's | 8% | 27% |

Table 8.1 shows some further elements of the political and business world of women in 1971. This was indeed the water they swam in, and highlights the potentials in place for women in 1971 versus those in 2005.

And finally, Table 8.2 shows are further elements of the social/educational/economic status of women over a 50-year time frame, 1970 versus current times (2020).

Adult female millennials have indeed looked out into a significantly expanded horizon compared to their female boomer predecessors. Standing upon the shoulders of the feminist boomers, millennials have been free to display more Lilith-like energies from the first creation story—a woman crafted from the same raw material as man who leans into an assumed expectation of equality.

As noted in the discussion of the boomers, no generation is monolithic in its character or its impact; nonetheless, we see hope embedded within millennials' overall agitation/anxiety as they are ascending to a greater cultural influence. Compared to the boomers, millennials are a more diverse generation in terms of race, sexuality, and gender identity (and Gen Z even more so). They carry a wider and deeper presumption of diversity, not only at work, but everywhere. This assumption seems paired with their expectation of essential fairness and social justice—while also reflecting impatience with the fact that America even still argues over who can be "excessed" from such consideration! The millennial generation is pushing and shifting the social discourse toward understanding the costs of adhering to a fixed binary identity. (To be explored in Chapter 12.) The 2022 Supreme Court's Dobbs decision has electrified female voter registration; millennial voter turnout is anticipated to be high beyond 2022 mid-term elections, given the loss of bodily autonomy, choice, and the patriarchal Dobbs court decision constituting a complete affront to their social values. This newest largest generation is, and will be, saying that it will not stand for this, that more change is needed, and that it will be coming.

The words of millennial New York Congresswoman Alexandria Ocasio-Cortez (AOC) capture well one political version of the millennial spirit of directness: "A lot of my dissent within the Democratic party comes from my lived experience. It's not just that we can be better, it's that we *have* to be better. We're not good enough right now."[39] In America's current state of polarization—what that "better" actually means, however, depends at this point almost entirely upon political party affiliation.

## In Summary

### *Points of Light and Shadow: Boomers To Millennials*

Boomer women, by and large, could not envision a professional life beyond primary or secondary school teaching, nursing, or secretarial work. These were the expected venues for working women in 1971. To put it metaphorically, the boomer women inherited the position of Eve, who was created from the rib of Adam, and was therefore, by definition, lesser. And yet, Eve was not content to simply accept what was her station in Paradise. She did reach for more, only to be punished thereafter for leaving her assigned place of companionship to Adam. Boomers' mothers had been invited into society to participate in full measure during the Second World War, only to be sent home afterward to their assigned place when their men came home. For the boomers, the question was left—what does it mean to be a woman anyway, and what can she do or become in America?

From a look at these two generations, the millennials are moving with unbridled speed away from the energies of Eve—to outright refusing to be limited by gender-assigned places or by roles defined by their relationships to men. They may or may not call themselves feminists, but essentially as a group, they appear to be so.

Millennials now have the opportunity to move the needle further and in larger steps—not only for feministic aims—but for the progress of humanism in general. They are also positioned to bring into focus the heretofore out-of-focus influence of the unconscious mind upon cultural currents—an influence which is so poorly appreciated in current society, but is at this point becoming more visible and accessible on the horizons of this century. It is because of this potentially pivotal work that this reflection and "call to arms" is especially, but not solely, aimed toward them.

Millennials have implicitly, if not explicitly, identified with energies of that "other" first woman, Lilith, inviting, as it were, a return of the repressed in womankind. In their feminism of this twenty-first century, we see a long-needed element of feminism appearing. Rather than only one face of feminism turned consciously upward toward the breaking of a "glass ceiling," there is in the millennials also a turning of their faces inward, looking to acknowledge and bring in the unconscious parts of sexism and putting these parts in active relationship to their own, and society's, conscious mind. Again, we share the direct voice of millennial legislator Alexandria Ocasio-Cortez (AOC): "My experience has given me a front row seat to how deeply and *unconsciously*, as well as consciously, so many people in this country hate women. And they hate women of color." And it's not just the right wing. Misogyny transcends political ideology left, right, center. This grip of patriarchy affects all of us, not just women, but men, as well. As mentioned before, ideologically there's an extraordinary lack of self-awareness in so many places.[40] In naming the Unconscious here, AOC unknowingly speaks an enduring truth—if you can't name it, you can't change it.

Thus, Lilith's metaphorical return and the shift in energies she brings to the equation of feminism in the millennial generation (we anticipate more in Gen Z) is only one way of marking what we hope is a broader cultural shift in the making. As this shift occurs, individual and societal accountability will take on more comprehensive meaning and requires more layered responses/interventions acknowledging and redressing years of unconscious bias and discrimination.

And finally, to return to the earlier words of AOC echoing "we have to do better", we wonder now *how and what* millennial leaders might leverage from two of the boomer generation's most prominent women leaders who worked devotedly in their own ways to make things "better" for all. In the next chapter therefore, we "talk story" about the two boomer-aged female leaders, Hillary Clinton and Angela Merkel.[41]

## Notes

1 From "The Living Years" by B. A. Robertson, and M. Rutherford (1988). This song was released when the earliest boomers were in their 30s and millennials were in latency childhood. Some early millennials had boomer parents, while later ones had Gen X or Generation Jones (those born between 1954 and 1965, like Obama) parents.
2 See National Archives (2008) data.
3 See Kao (2000).
4 Sexual revolution has had both its supporters and critique, i.e., it did not fully develop female sexuality on its own terms, and over the decades, the divorce rate has risen to raise questions about viability of "open relationships" or of monogamy itself.
5 This group of boomers pursued self-awareness and mind expansion with these drugs; and it is of note, some 50 years later, that the illegal, mind-altering drugs of marijuana, psilocybin, and LSD and MDM have either been legalized or are widely researched for use in medical and mental health treatments. Institutions conducting such research include Johns Hopkins, University of California, Berkely, NYU, Mount Sanai, Massachusetts General Hospital and the University of Wisconsin. And while all these generations under discussion have used alcohol

and marijuana more than other drugs, millennials stand out in their use of prescription painkillers, abusing them twice as much (at peak usage) than either their Gen X or boomer counterparts. See longitudinal data available via the National Survey on Drug Use and Health (NSDUH) and SAMHSA (2021).

6  We see this in the article by Perlman (2019) on drug use among middle-aged and older adults among other reports.

7  Dropping out as in hippie communes, but also in the form of withdrawal from political engagement and business careers, instead moving toward education and non-profits.

8  The Kent State shootings were the final straw for some, leading them to withdraw from the field of political action. Others were galvanized and inspired to do that much more.

9  Robert Putnam (2022), in a wide-ranging inclusive analysis, speaks to much of our own lived experiences. He also offers an historical review and projection as to how America might move—again—away from polarizing "Is" to more of an inclusive "We" in our national perspective. See earlier Putnam (2015) for analysis of how society has been failing children and proposed changes to support families, parents especially, education programs, and community supports.

10  See Slozar (2009) for an exploration of narcissism.

11  See Barshay (2021).

12  See Mishel and Kandra (2021).

13  Hugely wealthy, Bill Gates of Microsoft, did also become a huge philanthropist; Steve Jobs of Apple did not, but his widow Lauren Jobs has very much done so with her establishment of the Emerson Foundation. Interesting and balancing marital caveat.

14  See Siripurapu (2022).

15  Federal Reserve (2023) data indicates that as of Q4 2021, the top 1% of households in the United States held 32.3% of the country's wealth, while the bottom 50% held 2.6%. In 1928, in the US, the top 10% of earners captured 46% of the nation's income.

16  Thomas Piketty (2022) looking at the world's inequities has suggested a foot up for every individual into adulthood as a means to re-distribute wealth more fairly. What would happen if every person at age 25 was given an initial "universal capital endowment" funded by taxes on wealth and inheritances?!

17  See Federal Reserve (2023) data.

18  The ending of the Cold War and fall of the Berlin Wall symbolized, and perhaps fueled, an inflated fantasy of how both capitalism wedded with democracy would win the world over!

19  According to Columbia University Center on Poverty and Social Policy (2023), monthly poverty remained elevated in February 2022, with a 14.4% poverty rate for the total US population.

20  See Hare (1999).

21  See Sternberg (2019).

22  From the song "Constant Craving" by K. D. Lang, K.D. and Ben Mink (1992).

23  See the work of Twenge (2014).

24  See Stein (2013) for a more in-depth discussion of this.

25  See Glasmeier (2023) on living versus minimum wage for analysis of low-income block grant funding's steady decline.

26  See Callahan (2004).

27  Also trending has been decades of "grade inflation"—bringing a devaluing upon education itself. In parallel, liberal arts curricula have been devalued in comparison to those subjects that have a direct line to significant money-making immediately post-graduation. As experienced by both authors, students now often feel free and in fact "entitled" to pressure their teachers for an A—based not on what their actual performance is—but on what they perceive to be their own effort. A permutation of this trend is seen in young workers of "start-ups" who can expect that they should make it big/rich putting in just a few years' worth of work—even when they are not one of the founding creative principals!

28  See Allen et al. (2019), Ng et al. (2012), and van Ingen et al. (2015).

29  See Huddleston (2022).

30  See Mitchell (2022a). As an important aside, President Biden's aim to forgive up to $20,000 of college loans—currently shouldered by majority women and people of color—was scuttled by SCOTUS June 2023! See also Kent and Ado (2022).

31  See data collected from the Census and Federal Reserve (2023) as analyzed by Mitchell (2022b) in self.inc's "How big is the generational wealth gap in America?".

32  This is seen in Zuckerberg's re-naming and re-adjusting the financial structure of Facebook with aggressive moves to buy metaverse apps, as well as Microsoft, Apple, and Google all pouring resources in this direction.

33  See Statista Research Department's (2022) data.

34  See *Education Week*'s (2021) article.

35  See World Wildlife Fund (2022) & Reed (2020).

36  For information on trends around women in various political and professional roles, see the following:

Seats in Congress: History of Women in the US Congress (n.d.)
State Governorships: Pew Research Center (2018)
Fortune 500 CEOs: Catalyst (2019)
Network news anchors/co-anchors: P. Farhi (2006)
Attorneys: E. Michelson (2013)
MDs: M. Broxterman (2000) and Association of American Medical Colleges (2019)

37  See Cima (2017). Most of the movement toward gender parity occurred in the 1990s. In literature, parity was achieved around the 2000s. Gender bias persists still, however, in who gets reviewed in major publications. By 2005, with the advent of the internet, Facebook, and blogging, women of all ages now had access to write any time to any size interested audience without editorial evaluation or gender bias in selection—with a few bloggers either making a living (13% in 2021) or some side income (24%). By 2021, 77% of internet users read blogs everyday—where currently there is a gender-neutral distribution of bloggers. In 2020, there were 31.7 million bloggers in the US—people need to express themselves!

38  See US Bureau of Labor Statistics (2017) data.

39  See Fredrickson (2020, p.89). Also. Schuller (2021) for a contrast between millennials like AOC—where emphasis is on working for change from "bottom up"; and that of former Facebook executive Sheryl Sandberg in her book, *Lean In* (2013).

40  See Lowery. (2022) for extensive interview with AOC.

41  To "talk story" is an expression used in Hawaii for talking informally together.

## References

American Addiction Centers Editorial Staff (2018). Drug and alcohol abuse across generations. DrugAbuse.com, Updated June 30, 2023. https://drugabuse.com/featured/drug-and-alcohol-abuse-across-generations/

Allen, R., Allen, D., Karl, K. et al. (2019). Are millennials really an entitled generation? An investigation into generational equity sensitivity differences. ResearchGate.net, April. https://www.researchgate.net/publication/332153330_Are_Millennials_Really_an_Entitled_Generation_An_Investigation_into_Generational_Equity_Sensitivity_Differences

Association of American Medical Colleges (2019). Figure 12. Percentage of US medical school graduates by sex, academic years 1980–1981 through 2018–2019. AAMC. org. https://www.aamc.org/data-reports/workforce/data/figure-12-percentage-us-medical-school-graduates-sex-academic-years-1980-1981-through-2018-2019

Barshay, J. (2021). Proof points: The number of college graduates in the humanities drops for the eighth consecutive year. *The Hechinger Report*, November 22. https://hechingerreport.org/proof-points-the-number-of-college-graduates-in-the-humanities-drops-for-the-eighth-consecutive-year/

Broxterman, M. (2000). *Physician Statistics Summary (1970–1999)*. Pinnacle Health Group, January 3. https://www.phg.com/2000/01/physician-statistics-summary/

Callahan, D. (2004). *The Cheating Culture: Why More Americans Are Doing Wrong to Get Ahead*. Harper Collins.

Center for American Women and Politics (CAWP). History of Women in the US Congress. (n.d.). Cawp.rutgers.edu. https://cawp.rutgers.edu/facts/levels-office/congress/history-women-us-congress

Cima, R. (2017). *Bias, She Wrote*. The Pudding. https://pudding.cool/2017/06/best-sellers/

The Federal Reserve (2023). *Distribution of Household Wealth in the US Since 1989*. (Updated September 22.) https://www.federalreserve.gov/releases/z1/dataviz/dfa/distribute/table/

*Education Week* (2021). *School Shootings in 2021: How Many and Where*. edweek. org, March 1. https://www.edweek.org/leadership/school-shootings-this-year-how-many-and-where/2021/03

Farhi, P. (2006). New face of TV news first seen in the '70s. *Washington Post*, July 23. https://www.washingtonpost.com/archive/lifestyle/style/2006/07/23/new-face-of-tv-news-first-seen-in-the-70s/e5fd0c9e-6dfc-4534-bcba-3b9a8d25c4b5/

Fredrickson, C. (2020). *The AOC Way*. Sky Horse Publishing (p. 89).

Glasmeier, A. K. (2023) Living wage calculator. Massachusetts Institute of Technology. https://livingwage.mit.edu

Hare, R. (1999). *Without Conscience: The Disturbing World of the Psychopaths Among Us*. Guilford Publications.

Huddleston, T. (2022). Millennials and Gen Zers do want to buy homes—they just can't afford it, even as adults. CNBC report, June 12. www.cnbc.com/2022/06/12/millennials-and-gen-zers-want-to-buy-homes-but-they-cant-afford-it.html

Kao, A. (2000). History of oral contraception. *AMA Journal of Ethics*, 2(6). https://doi.org/10.1001/virtualmentor.2000.2.6.dykn1-0006.

Kent, A., & Ado, F. (2022). Gender and racial disparities in student loan debt. www.stlouisfed.org, November 10. https://www.stlouisfed.org/en/publications/economic-equity-insights/gender-racial-disparities-student-loan-debt#:~:text=Women%20(47%25)%20were%20more

Lang, K. D. & Mink, B. (1992). Constant Craving. On *Ingènue*. Words and music by K. D. Lang & Ben Mink. Copyright © 1992 Universal-Polygram International Publishing Inc., Bumstead Production U.S., INC and Zavion Enterprises, Inc. All Rights for BUMSTEAD PRODUCTIONS U.S., INC. Controlled and Administered by Universal-Polygram International Publishing, Inc. All Rights for Zavion Enterprises, Inc. Administered Worldwide by Kobalt Songs Music Publishing. All Rights Reserved. Used by Permission. *Reprinted by Permission of Hal Leonard LLC.*

Lowery, W. (2022). AOC on masculinity, power, and politics in post-Roe America. *GQ*, September 7. https://www.gq.com/story/alexandria-ocasio-cortez-october-cover-profile

Michelson, E. (2013). Women in the legal profession, 1970–2010: A study of the global supply of lawyers. *Indiana Journal of Global Legal Studies*, 20(2), 18. https://www.repository.law.indiana.edu/cgi/viewcontent.cgi?article=1531&context=ijgls

Mishel, L., & Kandra, J. (2021). Wage inequality continued to increase in 2020. Working Economics Blog; Economic Policy Institute, December 13. https://www.epi.org/blog/wage-inequality-continued-to-increase-in-2020-top-1-0-of-earners-see-wages-up-179-since-1979-while-share-of-wages-for-bottom-90-hits-new-low/

Mitchell, J. (2022a). *How Student Loans Became a National Catastrophe*. Simon & Schuster.

Mitchell, J. (2022b). Average net worth per generation (n.d.). www.self.inc, retrieved June 7, 2023. https://www.self.inc/info/generational-wealth-gap/#millennials

National Archives (2008). Vietnam War US military fatal casualty statistics. National Archives; The US National Archives and Records Administration, April 29. https://www.archives.gov/research/military/vietnam-war/casualty-statistics

National Center for Education Statistics (2021). *Digest of Education Statistics* (n.d.). Retrieved June 3, 2023, from https://nces.ed.gov/programs/digest/d21/tables/dt21_325.25.asp?current=yes

Ng, E., Lyons, S., & Schweitzer, L. (2012). *Managing the New Workforce*. Edward Elgar Publishing.

Parolin, Z., Collyer, S., & Curran, M. (2023). Monthly poverty in 2022 remains elevated in February. Columbia University Center on Poverty and Social Policy, Policy Brief, March 23. https://www.povertycenter.columbia.edu/publication/monthly-poverty-february-2022

Perlman, W. (2019). Drug use and its consequences increase among middle-aged and older adults. archives.nida.nih.gov, July 19. https://archives.nida.nih.gov/news-events/nida-notes/2019/07/drug-use-and-its-consequences-increase-among-middle-aged-and-older-adults

Pew Research Center. (2023, September 27). *The Data on Women Leaders*. Pew Research Center's Social & Demographic Trends Project. https://www.pewresearch.org/social-trends/fact-sheet/the-data-on-women-leaders.

Piketty, T. (2022). *Time for Socialism: Dispatches From a World on Fire: 2016–2021*. Yale University Press.

Putnam, R. (2015). *Our Kids: The American Dream in Crisis*. Simon & Schuster.

Putnam, R. (2022). *The Upswing: How America Came Together a Century Ago and How We Can Do It Again*. Simon and Schuster.

Robertson, B. A. and Rutherford, M. (1988). The Living Years. On *Living Years*. Music by Michael Rutherford and B. A. Robertson. Lyrics by B. A. Robertson.

Copyright © 1984, 1988 Concord Music Publishing LLC and R&BA Music Ltd. All Rights for R&BA Music Ltd. Administered by BMG Rights Management (US) LLC. All Right Reserved. Used by Permission. *Reprinted by Permission of Hal Leonard LLC.*

Rott, N. (2020). The world lost two-thirds of its wildlife in 50 years. We are to blame. NPR.org, September 10. https://www.npr.org/2020/09/10/911500907/the-world-lost-two-thirds-of-its-wildlife-in-50-years-we-are-to-blame

SAMHSA. (2021). *2021 National Survey of Drug Use and Health (NSDUH) Releases.* www.samhsa.gov. https://www.samhsa.gov/data/release/2021-national-survey-drug-use-and-health-nsduh-releases

Schuller, K. (2021). *The Trouble with White Women: A Counter-History Of Feminism.* Bold Type Books.

Siripurapu, A. (2022). The US Inequality Debate. Council on Foreign Relations, April 20. https://www.cfr.org/backgrounder/us-inequality-debate

Slozar, J. (2009). *The Culture of Excess: How America Lost Self-Control and Why We Need to Redefine Success.* Praeger: ABC-CLIO.

Smith, T. J., & Russell, K. (2023). The greatest wealth transfer in history is here, with familiar (rich) winners. *The New York Times,* May 14. https://www.nytimes.com/2023/05/14/business/economy/wealth-generations.html

Statista Research Department (2023). Number of K-12 school shootings in the in the United Stated from 1979 to June 2022, by active shooter status. Statista.com. https://www.statista.com/statistics/971473/number-k-12-school-shootings-us/

Stein, J. (2013). Millennials: The me me me generation. In *TIME,* May 20. https://time.com/247/millennials-the-me-me-me-generation/

Sternberg, J. C. (2019). *The Theft of a Decade.* Public Affairs.

Twenge, J. M. (2014). *Generation Me—Revised and Updated: Why Today's Young Americans Are More Confident, Assertive, Entitled—and More Miserable Than Ever Before.* Atria.

US Bureau of Labor Statistics (2017). *The Economics Daily: A Look at Women's Education and Earnings Since the 1970s.* bls.gov, December 27. https://www.bls.gov/opub/ted/2017/a-look-at-womens-education-and-earnings-since-the-1970s.htm

van Ingen, D. J., Freiheit, S. R., Steinfeldt, J. A. et al. (2015). Helicopter parenting: The effect of an overbearing caregiving style on peer attachment and self-efficacy. *Journal of College Counseling, 18*(1), 7–20. https://doi.org/10.1002/j.2161-1882.2015.00065.x

World Wildlife Fund (2022). *Living Planet Report.* October 14.

# Chapter 9

# Flight Paths
## Hillary Clinton and Angela Merkel

The universe may be made of quantum particles, but our world is made of those many bits called letters that become our stories.

Psychology and our everyday experiences tell us that people seek—and *need*—to idealize selected others, for inspiration, for love, etc. We all have such figures, often people in leadership positions, in our families, schools, entertainment, sports, politics. And yet, to over-idealize someone is to shear them of their basic humanity, being the complex and limited human beings that they in fact are. Foundational to that human condition are their own particular unconscious forces, the foibles of their temperament, the personal deficits carved through personal developmental history, etc. These things do not necessarily make them a less successful leader—but indeed, make them more relatable. For example, Hillary Clinton was criticized in the 1990s for not leaving her husband in response to his infidelity, as if to accept his imperfection nullified her leadership capacities. Similarly, the millennial Congresswoman, Alexandria Ocasio Cortez, was criticized simply for attending the Met Gala in 2021, and even more so because she wore a gown emblazoned with "Tax the Rich." Was she being hypocritical? Was she being disrespectful? On the other hand, could she not just have an evening of fun and still be a fierce advocate for others?!

No person is perfect, nor completely whole, but some individuals can be taken as modeling ideals for others in terms of their attitudes, thinking, and social actions. To date, were we to pick one model of a politically powerful and socially progressive woman as to idealize, it would be former House Speaker, Nancy Pelosi. Pelosi is of the "Greatest Generation", however, and she also carries a legacy from a political family.

But our focus here is on women of the boomer generation—two women who rose to leadership despite the challenges of systemic misogyny and racism within the context and parameters of their own individual lives. For many of us—anticipating a Clinton victory in the US presidential contest of 2016—we constructed the imagined picture of two women, for the first time in history, leading the Western democratic world: Hillary Clinton in America

DOI: 10.4324/9781032677309-11

and Angela Merkel in Germany. There was a comfort and confidence that the global fragmentation wrought in the twenty-first century by toxic nationalism and terrorism would be addressed by their combined female leadership in a manner that male leadership had been unable to achieve.

The stories of these two Western white female leaders of the boomer generation may be something that today's, and future, millennial political leaders may draw upon, or may push off from to find their own different strokes.

## Two Stories: Clinton and Merkel

These two short stories illustrate two women of a shared generation with similar traditional family backgrounds, but with very different educational training, and with quite different pathways to leadership in their respective democracies. Hillary Clinton has been a national leader in multiple political positions, but one who did not reach the highest executive office in the USA. Angela Merkel, who had a shorter history of political positions, was however, elected executive leader of Germany for multiple terms, serving her country for 16 years before she chose to step down.

Both women are white. Both sought executive leadership in democratic countries. Merkel grew up in a country with many more centuries of lived history and different forms of government. Clinton grew up in a younger country, but one with a longer living history of democratic government. There is something to be mined here—from both their similarities and differences—that could be useful for aspiring political leaders of our next largest generation—the millennials—whose leadership will likely be carried on the shoulders of a non-white woman.

### Women of a Feather

When looking at the routes Clinton and Merkel took into politics, there are obvious similarities as well as important differences. Arguably, Clinton is the most profiled female politician in America—evoking strong reactions—both positive and negative.[1] She has been in the public eye for decades. Much less is known about Merkel's early life, and although less written about, it has also stimulated both strong positive and negative reactions in others.[2] Would either person provoke such strong reactions if she were male? (We think not.)

Both Clinton and Merkel were the oldest child in a family with at least one younger brother. And yet, it appears that in both families, the parents' push for achievement focused more upon their daughters. In families with multiple children, it is often the first child who becomes the strongest achiever and the one most seeking of parental approval. We also know from social scientific research that when a father is involved beyond a traditional or culturally circumscribed paternal role, girls especially benefit in their push to transcend traditional female gender roles.[3] Both women had fathers who pushed them to be "the best." Indirectly, if not directly, the message was conveyed that gender was not necessarily a limiting factor. In fact, it has been noted that Merkel does not locate her strong sense of identity in her gender. Clinton did not employ the issue of her gender in her 2008 presidential run, but then pivoted in 2016 to do so.

Both Clinton and Merkel grew up in intact families which instilled values that were aligned with the ideals of their religious faith. The Rodham family's Methodist faith became a pillar of Clinton's personal identity and psychological stability. She has been strengthened by the undergirding of that faith when she has encountered disappointments in personal or professional realms. The Lutheran faith of Merkel's family also provided her a strong faith scaffolding that may be somewhat less apparent due to her training as a scientist and because she maintains a wide circle of privacy around her personal life. For both Clinton and Merkel, it could be said that their faith imparted to them an inherent sense of responsibility to and for others.

A critical difference in their families, however, was that Clinton's father, a small businessman, could be quite emotionally abusive and critical—toward both his wife and his children. While giving Hillary special attention—making her a "daddy's girl"—he did not attenuate his critical stance toward her. It is reported that he himself carried a depressive and somewhat bitter strain. It may be that his interpersonal criticism and aggression was rooted in his use of criticism as a defense against his own depression. Clinton is herself vulnerable to that same depression. And it appears that as an adult, Clinton may have refracted her experience of her father's criticalness by looking for external "enemies" to fight—those who were at variance with the strong values and ideals she championed. (Of course, her training in law—adversarial—both reflects and facilitates this mission.) In public, she primarily denies her father's hurtful aggression, transforming it into a positive: the establishing of high standards for herself to meet. This has, perhaps, left her somewhat more vulnerable to being protective of the frailties and excesses of the most significant men in her life.

In contrast, Merkel's father, a Lutheran pastor, was recognized and well respected in his community, although he is said to have been emotionally distant within the family itself. Home life was less complicated for Merkel—not being buffeted as much by the psychological issues of either parent. But there was family tension related to her father's moving the family from West to East Germany to take charge of a parsonage and to develop a college on a campus that had been formerly for people with mental health illnesses.

The Berlin Wall was built four years after their move, and a pervasive environment of surveillance enveloped them. The division of Germany into communist versus non-communist sections resulted in her mother's losing her career. The family was, however, joined in their solidarity with Western values. Relatives in America sent the family items that were unavailable, or even censored, in East Germany. As a result of their reserved family style, they were more able to have a life largely unobstructed by communist oversight. In sum, Merkel was able to internalize the support of her parents and to acquire a visible unselfconscious confidence in her thinking, values, and ability to discern the time and circumstances for speaking her mind.

A certain similarity exists in both their fathers' promotion of their daughter's talents and abilities. Similarly, their mothers were quite aware of the limits that social roles could impose on their daughters' desires. Clinton's mother had high hopes for her daughter—wanting very much for Hillary to achieve in a manner that had been inaccessible to herself. She imagined Hillary as a Supreme Court justice.

Merkel's mother had been a professional woman. She was a teacher but her ability to work was quashed when Germany was divided by communism. Merkel's mother's association-by-marriage to a pastor was the ostensible reason for this prohibition. Her mother, however, quickly returned to work after the fall of the Berlin Wall. In that respect, Angela had a model of her mother's being a professional woman, while at the same time, she witnessed how a woman's professional position could be utterly determined by her relationship to a man, or via governmental edict.

## Different Flight Paths: Education

Graduate education is where a significant divergence begins to emerge between Clinton and Merkel. Like many in America who aim to enter politics, Clinton attended law school. The investment in how the symbolic structure of law sets and changes social conditions is central to her thinking. In law school during her twenties, her lifelong commitment to children and family took root. In contrast, Merkel pursued science—quantum physics—because it offered her more freedom from communist state interference than most other fields, and it was also congruent with her own personal interest and aptitudes. Her years of living among children and adults with mental health problems, however, spawned in her a commitment to responsibility for disadvantaged others. As much as Merkel may have enjoyed her pursuit of science, she appears to have had little trouble leaving it for politics when the opportunity emerged! She took her well-trained, analytical mind with her, serving her well in her interactions with other party members or international political leaders. It is evident that the "feelings" variable so often evident in females and female leaders is not as prominent in her style as might be expected. She was 35 when the Berlin Wall came down and when talk of the reunification of Germany began. She immediately threw herself into politics. Thus, hers was a much later entry into the political scene than Clinton's, who was already involved in politics in her twenties.

Though both Clinton and Merkel could be said to be articulate thinkers and planners, the difference in graduate training shows through in their respective styles of thought. Clinton's thinking is filtered through the rule of law and how law can change social structures. Merkel thinks and listens as a scientist—variable by variable—generating multiple hypotheses, working out the arguments of each until she comes to a final conclusion, and then she fights for it. But she has also been criticized for "flip-flopping" on issues. This may be explained by her scientist's stance of shifting positions in the face of new data.

Clinton and Merkel both uphold the ideal of "making the world a better place." At their foundations is a profound sense of "responsibility for the other" which is expressed in their shared ideals of justice and freedom for all. It was no accident or simple political expediency that Clinton's 2016 election slogan was "Better Together." These shared values were also evident in Merkel's decision to take in more than a million Middle Eastern refugees in 2015—despite significant political and social resistance from the Right. It is the fact of these shared values that perhaps most accounts for their "being birds of a feather," holding onto and sustaining what many would label "feminine" values in the operation of government.

### Political Pathways

Hillary Clinton came upon the national political stage aged 22 via her provocative graduation speech at Wellesley in 1969. She was the president of her class. From then on, others began to frame her in terms of leadership and political significance. Her trajectory, however, was altered by her relationship to Bill Clinton, whom she met in law school and eventually married. Theirs was, and remains today from all accounts, a passionate and complicated partnership—pursuing deeply shared values and a vision for America. Soldered thus, Hillary, for many years, subordinated whatever executive leadership aspirations she had to supporting and strategizing Bill Clinton's career rising to, and through, the presidency. It was only nearing the end of the Clinton presidency that Clinton threw her own hat into the ring of election politics by running for, and winning, a Senate seat in the state of New York.

It is from the Senate that she launched her first run for the presidency—losing in 2008 to another charismatic Senator, Barack Obama. It is interesting to note that in this campaign for the Democratic nomination, she purposely avoided the topic of gender. Although losing to Obama, her star continued to brighten through accepting the leadership of the State Department in the Obama administration. Her work brought her to occupy the position of the most respected woman leader on the globe. The marital roles of who was supporting whom in the Clinton marriage appeared to reverse themselves. Nearing the end of Obama's second term, Hillary once again organized herself for the presidential election of 2016. This time she embraced the issue of gender—drawing on the historical significance of being the first woman to be a presidential nominee, with hopes for America to have its first woman president. Her decades of being in politics and in the public eye worked both for and against her. She, perhaps more than any other woman in America, for over 25 years had borne the hate, fear, and negative judgments foisted upon her by many, simply for being a woman in the public sphere with her own mind, her own ambitions, and her own ideals and ideas. We wonder now if Hillary Clinton symbolically and practically absorbed the misogyny that she suffered as a way to clear the field for subsequent women seeking the highest executive office of the US presidency.

For Angela Merkel, it has been a very different political arc. She was 35 when her political journey began, coincident with the fall of the Berlin Wall. She brought to the political marketplace whatever more lived experience happens between one's early 20s and mid 30s, accruing intellectual maturity and political savvy. Her ideas, fermenting in silence under a communist regime, emerged quickly when the Berlin Wall fell in 1989. As the sundry political parties began to form, she weighed the aims of them all. Ultimately, she chose the Christian Democratic Union party, whose guiding aim was to protect the inviolate dignity of each human being as embedded within twin values of freedom and justice. This party's platform clearly resonated with her family values. She took her place in a party of men—but then, she had already dealt with being the only female among men before in her field of physics. It was not long before her ability to analyze and articulate complex issues set her apart and onto a rising trajectory. Right away she was mentored by two powerful men—one after the other—who promoted her abilities. Her intuitive ability to strategize within a system of multiple parties also enabled her to use coalitions defensively and assertively toward her party's aims and her own ambitions. Merkel by all measures catapulted into German politics and rose to the Chancellorship in a short 15 years' time. She remained in the Chancellorship for 16 years—and has been the only chancellor to leave voluntarily (versus by election loss), announcing in 2018 she would not seek office again.

Early on their political path, both Clinton and Merkel worked with, or for, children. Clinton also had a child and struggled with the common dilemma of the demands of career and motherhood, while Merkel did not. A question this comparison raises is whether it is easier to hold and care for all the babies when you do not have one of your own to raise. Perhaps even when a woman does not bear a child, due to that built-in place/space for another in her body, there is corresponding space in her mind to consider the responsibility to another.[4]

Both Merkel and Clinton established early on a few key supporters and close colleagues who accompanied them over the entire arc of their political trajectories. This intentional interpersonal webbing of trust has enabled each of them in their reach into more powerful, but also more precarious, political positions over time.

### Salient Socio-Political Differences

There is an inherent difference between the US and Germany, worth considering when looking at Merkel's success and Clinton's failure in reaching the highest office of the land. Germany has been an organized country for many more centuries than America—during which, for some of that time, women have held national leadership. Also, their current social policies support a work/family balance which enables greater gender equality and more of a platform for women to pursue politics. In contrast, America is a much younger country, having no history of female executive leadership. America has been a working democratic structure much longer than Germany. (Germany as a democracy was re-established in a re-united Germany after the fall of the Berlin Wall in 1989. Previously, between 1918 and 1933, Germany had been a democracy, but from 1933 to 1945, was a dictatorship under Hitler, followed by a divided Germany: between the democratic West Germany and a communist East Germany, up until 1990.) Either way, one country has a history of intermittent female leadership and the other country does not. Does this make for any less unconscious sexism in Germany than in the US?

There may be another unconscious factor at play that rarely, if ever, gets confronted in national or global politics concerning Merkel's rise to executive leadership and/or Clinton's inability to crack the glass ceiling. It revolves around this question: How does a country deal with its own unconscious destructive elements and group aggression?

Simply put, dehumanizing others frees one's own aggression to be expressed without needing to take responsibility for one's destructive actions and their consequences. Because all human beings have both an unconscious as well as conscious mind, there is a ubiquitous human tendency to project unwanted negative, weak, and feared parts of ourselves upon others, and then to persecute those selected others as somehow less than human. This is a simple psychological truth that is hard to acknowledge and hard to accept as a basic existential reality that belongs to the human condition. But it does.

In America, the unconscious destructive elements of our racist past, and the remaining vestiges of it, have not been sufficiently acknowledged and have not been sufficiently integrated into our view of ourselves as a nation. This lack of acknowledgement and integration is core to our national DNA, reflected in the very founding documents of our American democracy. Constitutional amendments and federal and state laws are our ongoing efforts to make this "a more perfect union," but there is a different kind of psychological work that remains to be done. A collective acknowledgement and integration of the dark side of this nation, both historically and in current times, would involve, in part, the active effort to bring into conscious representation (via words and art) what is and/or has been the vast field of unspeakable historical actions that American society would rather keep denying or outright repress. Large unintegrated pieces involve our initial theft from and excessing of the Indigenous American peoples, the building of our country on the backs of enslaved Africans, answering the thirteenth, fourteenth and fifteenth amendments with Jim Crow laws of segregation, and finally the actual, and psychological, terrorism directed for over 200 years toward Black and all non-white people in America. The NY Times 1619 Project has represented a significant effort in this direction—but it has also generated intense social backlash among a segment of America.[5]

In this respect, it is Germany that offers a model of integration. Article 1 of the German Constitution simply proclaims, "Human dignity shall be inviolable." This short, simple sentence was Germany's answer to the catastrophe that was the Second World War, to the murder of six million Jews in the Holocaust, to the hate, destruction, and annihilation that Germany brought to Europe and to the world.

Germany has actively (despite its ever-present human ambivalence) gone about the work of "working through" the dark shadow of Nazism[6] and anti-Semitism in its culture and history, using art and words to integrate its past darkness into its national group identity. There is truth-telling—where children are taught in school about Nazism's human cost. There are many small visible markers on German streets of human lives lost to Nazism. There are big and small monuments. There is not only the psychological and concrete work of reparation, but also the slow, difficult work of acknowledging responsibility by the perpetrators of such dehumanizing aggression.[7] There are national days of remembrance. In addition, financial reparations have been made over decades to survivors of the Holocaust and the forced laborers of the Second World War.

Too often Germany is used as a scapegoat for Western countries to project their darker elements onto, as if to say, "Something like Nazism could never happen here." And yet, we elected Donald Trump, who has systematically fomented racial hatred and violence during and after his administration. And those in his contrails, like Governor Ron DeSantis of Florida, reach forward with an eerily identical agenda. The aftermath of "Trumpism" has become like a fog crossing the San Francisco Bay that has enveloped most of the Republican party. We have a choice. We could become the Germany of Nazism and the Second World War, or we could become more like the current Germany that, over decades of on and off psychological work, strives to come to terms with its Holocaust.[8]

America has yet to really do the same with our own history. In fact, currently a major political conflict is whether we will, or will not, have truth-telling in our schools and teach our children about American racism as told, for example, by the 1619 Project. We have yet to ask what anti-racist efforts remain necessary to remedy this boulevard of human suffering. The removal of Confederate flags over government property, the removal of

Confederate monuments, the establishment of an art project marking places of past lynchings and slave auctions are all important examples of a "working through" effort.[9] And still, it is also worth noting that the National Museum of African-American History and Culture, opened in 2016, was the very last Smithsonian museum, built on the very last piece of federal land designated for these museums. (This land had previously been farmed by slaves for government officials.) Reparations for slavery and subsequent policies limiting Black people's opportunities for education, work, housing, and wealth accumulation have been taken up for study, recommendations, or actual implementation of reparations by select states (California) and certain localities (Ashville, NC) when the reality is that a federal solution is required to be adequate to the lived history. And we have yet to face our blood debt to Indigenous peoples. We have yet to own all of the expressions of white supremacy that stain our American conscience. We have yet to pay women equal salary for equal work. We both (authors) have mothers who were born before American women had the right to vote.

So, is there any relationship between the ongoing psychological work of German society to deal with the dark side of its unconscious—expressed in Nazism—and their willingness to put its welfare repeatedly in the hands of a woman for 16 years?

Today in 2023, as polarization and white nationalism have increased in America, Merkel's 2009 words to the US Congress, concerning the difficulties of globalization highlighted in right-wing populism in both US and Germany, are prescient …

"It is our duty to convince people that globalization is an immense global opportunity, for each continent, because it forces us to act together with others. The alternative to globalization would be shutting ourselves off from others, but this is not a viable alternative. It would lead only to isolation and therefore misery. Thinking in terms of alliances and partnerships, on the other hand, is what will take us into a good future."

### In Closing

When America can speak in the way of Germany to itself and the world—and—perhaps in the future, when we can elect a Black woman president—we will know something huge will have shifted in our collective identity. America needs many more women in positions of political power to get us there by bringing in more of the feminine values and ideas shared by Clinton and Merkel.

Depending upon one's perspective regarding America's presidential election structure—in 2016 Clinton lost the presidential election via the electoral college or, in 2016, Clinton won the majority of voters by three million votes. Yet that election was never just about a woman's losing again to a man. It was a very "group-conscious" woman losing to a self-involved man of multiple excesses who lives outside the envelope of human empathy—and as outside the law—as he can. Despite Trump's loss of both the electoral college and popular vote in 2020, his psychic plantings in excess within his brittle personality structure have meant that external reality has been replaced with delusional "big lie(s)"—that too many others have grasped as their own. America has sent itself very strong messages in Trump's winning—and in his losing—of the presidency. This excess upon excess beckons to be more fully examined and answered to. Hopefully, America is experiencing its last patriarchal gasp of toxic masculinity. If America does not hold Trump finally legally accountable for his actions and words, or clings to a that hope he, and the others mirroring him, will disappear by the 2024 election, we do so at our own peril.

In the 1976 movie *Network*, there is a compelling scene of resistance pertinent this moment.[10] The main character—a commentor of a news/entertainment TV program—leans out his office window and yells into the darkness of his city that he is so damn mad that he is not going to take "this" anymore. It is a direct call to arms, and about which the "this" is not entirely clear. Voices cascade and response builds throughout his city as more and more citizens lean out their windows yelling the same refrain—"I'm so mad I'm not going to take this anymore." Imagine if you will, this is Hillary Clinton in her continuing "warrior work" leaning out that window yelling—"I'm so mad that *we're* not going to take this anymore." Because today, for all women—but especially millennial and Gen Z women—the "this" is their right to bodily autonomy and their right to choose their future—and they are "damn mad." Their robust voting in the 2022 mid-term election is just the first registration of their power. For all democracy-believing others, the "this" represents the insurrectionist words and actions that threaten to bring autocracy clearly in view through the smoke and flames of a Capitol burning—and "we" *ought not* "take it anymore." Let these excesses be a foreshadow of heralding, and not a harbinger, of things to come.

## Notes

1  See Bernstein (2008), Clinton (2014), and Bond (2015).
2  See authorized biography by Marton (2021) and Kornelius. (2014). Also, the (2022) Netflix documentary *Merkel: Macht Der Freiheit.*
3  See Mao et al. (2020) and McLanahan et al. (2013).
4  There is no implication here that it is necessary that a person have a womb to have that consideration in their mind, but merely a wonder of whether there is a trace of biological fertility in the mental map of the mind.
5  See Hannah-Jones et al. (2019).
6  This reparative process was begun in 1951 by Chancellor Adenauer and added to in 1990 when Germany was re-unified. The Article 2 Fund continued reparations and the project of "truth telling" with "days of remembrance."

7 See Bohleber (2019) for his discussion of traumatic states in survivors of the Holocaust regarding the attack on the psyche's ability to make meaning, hold onto any empathy, or maintain any internal representation of a "good object" (person). Unprocessed trauma becomes transmitted across generations—living like foreign objects within that still need psychic processing. At the group/collective level or on an individual level, the human cost and effort required to psychically move through trauma states is similar.

8 See Smith (2022) for a good summary of Germany's reckoning and healing process and with thoughts on America's parallel path—also, his book (2021) has excellent personal reporting on different US places of slavery in the past, and what and how these places do or do not engage with that history.

9 A number of additional present-day projects are doing similar societal work. The National Memorial for Peace and Justice in Montgomery, Alabama (among others across the nation) are making lynching sites more visible to the general public. The *Washington Post* reported on and brought to the light how many Congressmen in American history owned slaves. Various universities are acknowledging and making reparations for their own participation in slavery. These are all works that bring the repressed past into our collective consciousness.

10 Sidney Lumet (1976). The film received many awards. It captured a certain zeitgeist of capitalism and was very prescient of what cable TV and the world situation vis-à-vis terrorism would become in the following decades.

## References

Bernstein, C. (2008). *A Woman In Charge: The Life of Hillary Rodham Clinton*. Arrow.

Bohleber, W. (2019). *Destructiveness, Intersubjectivity and Trauma: The Identity Crisis of Modern Psychoanalysis*. Routledge.

Bond, A. H. (2015). *Hillary Rodham Clinton: On The Couch*. Bancroft Press.

Clinton, H. R. (2014). *Hard Choices: A Hillary Rodham Clinton New Memoir*. New York Simon & Schuster.

Hannah-Jones, N., Elliott, M., & Hughes, J. (2019). *The 1619 Project*. New York Times. New York Times Company, & Smithsonian Institution.

Kornelius, S. (2014). *Angela Merkel: The Authorized Biography*. Alma Books.

Lumet, S. (dir.) (1976). *Network*. USA, MGM Studio. 0:55:15-46. "I'm mad as hell, and I'm not going to take this anymore."

Mao, M., Zang, L., & Zhang, H. (2020). The effects of parental absence on children development: Evidence from left-behind children in China. *International Journal of Environmental Research and Public Health*, 17(18), 6770. https://doi.org/10.3390/ijerph17186770

Marton, K. (2021) *The Chancellor: The Remarkable Odyssey of Angela Merkel*. Simon & Schuster.

McLanahan, S., Tach, L., & Schneider, D. (2013). The causal effects of father absence. *Annual Review of Sociology*, 39, 399–427. https://doi.org/10.1146/annurev-soc-071312-145704

Netflix documentary (2022). *Merkel: Macht Der Freiheit*.

Smith, C. (2021). *How The Word is Passed: A Reckoning with the History of Slavery Across America*. Dialogue Books.

Smith, C. (2022). *Monuments to the Unthinkable*. The Atlantic, November 14. https://www.theatlantic.com/magazine/archive/2022/12/holocaust-remembrance-lessons-america/671893/

# Chapter 10

# Warrior Work
## Ground Zero—ERA Passage

### Call to Arms

Looking back at the January 21, 2017's Women's March protesting Donald Trump's election to the US presidency, it was nothing if not a "call to arms" to all feminists—of all genders. This 2017 protest was the *biggest* protest *ever* in US history—and, perhaps, the most racially and generationally diverse of all feminist efforts to date.[1]

It indeed symbolized the gathering of arms for a fight. But it was also about linking arms together. In this event, the white women who did not vote for Trump joined forces with the overwhelming percentage of Black women who had cast their votes for Hillary Clinton. Predicted by many to be the candidate who would finally break the ultimate glass ceiling, Hillary did not.

In response to this "call to arms," women took to the political arena in large numbers in the 2018 elections. In 2018, more women (including white women, women of color, and LGBTQ candidates) ran for, and won, political office at both local and national levels than ever before.[2] Unfortunately, the insurrection of January 6, 2021 dropped a pall of fear over members of Congress—especially women of color—who have suffered threats to their welfare—even by their own Congressional colleagues! In the ensuing years, the fog of Trumpism has spread, unabated, feeding the delusion of the "big lie" and encouraging Make American Great Again (MAGA) candidates to enter Congressional as well as Secretary of State-level races for the 2022 mid-terms.

### The Equal Rights Amendment

There are many arenas where continued resistance to sexism, racism, and misogyny is needed. But one stands out as particularly salient at this time, in this century. The legislation of equal rights for a full 50% of the population would seem to be a compelling agenda. In 2014, when Supreme Court Justice Ruth Bader Ginsburg was asked how the US Constitution should be amended, she responded succinctly: "Passage of the Equal Rights Amendment." Amending

DOI: 10.4324/9781032677309-12

the US Constitution to protect the rights of women by affirming the basic ground of equal human rights would fill in a Constitutional gap—the silent assignment of women to a less-than status—left by the Founding Fathers since 1789.

In 2018, Senator Kamala Harris engaged with Supreme Court nominee Brett Kavanaugh as follows: "Can you think of any laws that give the government power to make decisions about the male body?" So de-centered by such a question challenging white male privilege, Kavanaugh was rendered speechless. The question had to be repeated before Kavanaugh could offer his very stumbling answer of, "No."

This brief 2018 exchange between Senator Harris and nominee Kavanaugh illustrates the inherent blindness of unconscious sexism in America, and the need to recognize and address gender inequality legislatively. Yet, here we are in 2023 having gone backward! Women are once again forbidden ownership of their own bodies and legally prevented from making choices concerning their own futures, should an unexpected and unwanted pregnancy occur![3]

The equal rights amendment, initially introduced as a constitutional amendment in 1923, clearly and simply codifies the following:

"**Section 1.** Equality of rights under the law shall not be denied or abridged by the United States or by any State on account of sex.

**Section 2.** The Congress shall have the power to enforce, by appropriate legislation, the provisions of this article.

**Section 3.** This amendment shall take effect two years after the date of ratification."

President John Adams is credited with saying that the American Revolution is not truly won until all slaves are free. Can we not also say that the American Revolution is not truly won until there is true both racial *and* gender equality?[4] Society's language of law lands upon human bodies and minds, shaping, limiting, and/or freeing the bodies and minds of its citizenry. It took seven generations of women's activism to secure the right to vote. Nearly 100 years after its inception, we are still without ratification of the Equal Rights Amendment.

The Equal Rights Amendment has had a rocky history. It was initially introduced in 1923, three years after women's right to vote was ratified. For decades, it went nowhere. But in 1970, Democratic Representative Martha Griffiths brought the amendment to the floor of the US House, where it passed. It passed in the House on October 12, 1971, and in the Senate on March 22, 1972. What remained was ratification by three-quarters (38) of the 50 states. There was a seven-year time limit imposed on such passage. In the next two years, 33 states ratified the amendment, while according to

Gallup's polling, 75% of the population supported it. In 1979, the seven-year deadline for ratification came due and was extended by three years to 1982. Still, when that deadline arrived, only 35 states had passed the amendment—three states short of the majority required by the Constitution.

This failure was followed by another 35-year time-lapse. Then, in March 2017, the state of Nevada became the 36th state to ratify the Equal Rights Amendment. This was quickly followed by the state of Illinois, which became the 37th state to ratify the ERA in April 2018. On January 27, 2020, the state of Virginia made history by becoming the 38th state to ratify the ERA. But, even before Virginia ratified the ERA, the Trump-era Department of Justice's Office of Legal Counsel (OLC) issued a 38-page opinion arguing that the three recent ratifications were invalid because they came too late. The Attorneys General from the three final states to ratify—Nevada, Illinois and Virginia—filed suit to require the archivist to certify the ERA. Finally, in 2022, the newly elected Attorney General of Virginia halted the legal campaign to push the federal government to recognize Virginia's 2020 ratification, and there the amendment died, once again ...[5]

Meanwhile, after multiple legislative attempts in 2020, the US House of Representatives passed legislation saying there should be no time limit on the question of ratifying the ERA. The 2021 bill did not pass the Senate because all the Democratic senators and at least ten Republicans would be needed for its passage. Then in April 2023, the Republican Senate defeated, again, another joint resolution calling for an end to any time limit on ERA passage.

So, what is in the ERA that is so controversial that half the population of America is denied equal rights?

Article 5 of the US Constitution sets out two requirements for amendments: approval by two-thirds of both chambers of Congress and ratification by three-quarters (38) of the states. On January 27, 2020, the Equal Rights Amendment finally achieved both of these requirements, but the Trump administration blocked the certification and publication of the amendment. Constitutional law scholars dispute that a seven-year timeline for ratification in the preamble to the ERA passed by Congress in 1972 means that recent ratifications are invalid. "States did not vote for the timeline—states voted for the text of the ERA. The timeline was in a preamble. The timeline is definitely not binding on Congress," said Georgetown law professor Victoria Nourse.

Legal scholars argue that it is likely that Congress has the power to legislatively adjust or remove the time limit constraint on the ERA if it chooses, to determine whether or not state ratifications which occur after the expiration of a time limit in a proposing clause are valid, and to promulgate the ERA after the 38th state ratifies. Attention is now directed to the fight for Congress to remove the deadline. Sister bills are active in both the Senate and House of Representatives.

For some, the ERA is seen as a relic of the 1970s social movements and "we should just move on." The fact is, however, that America cannot really move forward as a "just nation" without it. In 2022, according to the SDG Gender Index (tracking began in 2015), the *United States ranked 38th in the world in terms of gender equality.* Tracking girls and women across multiple categories—health and work, as examples—*the US is significantly closer in rank to less wealthy nations than its counterparts.* (For context though, as of 2022, no country has achieved complete gender parity!)[6]

The simple wording of the ERA would guarantee missing protections and equality mandates in multiple arenas of American life. Protections, access, and legal support that women have had to fight for on a piece-by-piece basis (e.g., the right to vote, the right to their own credit cards, the right to own property, the right not to be fired for being pregnant, the right to be free of sexual harassment at work) would be protected wholesale and all at once.

## The Dobbs Decision

Beyond the argument of how much the implementation of the ERA would cost in dollars, significant opposition to its passage has always been fueled by anti-abortion advocates who have recently won their 50-year battle in Dobbs' Supreme Court's 2022 anti-abortion ruling. This makes passage of the ERA even more crucial. The ERA would require medical access for equality in the array of reproductive services.[7] Stripping women of their reproductive fiat has effectively reduced women, both consciously and unconsciously, to the position of being a designated reproductive vessel for the replenishment of society. The rank hypocrisy of the pro-life movement is clearly illustrated by the lack of social structures supporting mothers and children—especially in those states which eschew expanding Medicaid (most often in Red versus Blue states).[8]

Furthermore, why should pregnancy be solely a woman's responsibility? It takes two to do that particular tango. It's as though women's engagement is proscribed, but men's is freely sanctioned. Why is that "just the way it is"?

*In this present moment in history, access to abortion should rest less on "reproductive rights" and more on the ground zero of "reproductive justice."* The number of women's lives that will be put in danger of death by this ruling essentially puts passage of the ERA in the territory of a high stakes game, with death as its ante.

And, let us call a spade a spade. The US government ought to establish a male pro-life registry of DNA samples of males from birth. It should be established by the same court or Congress that requires a woman to carry a pregnancy to full term. For this registry, a DNA sample would be taken from every birthed genetic male so paternity can be checked whenever there is a pregnancy. If a 12-year-old pregnant girl will now be forced to carry a fetus to term, then the biological father of this pregnancy—or his parents—should be legally responsible to pick up the requisite tab of financial responsibility for a child born, starting from birth and reaching all the way to age 26 years. The financial burden should fall equally on the two parents of that life; but none of that is touched on in the SCOTUS (Supreme Court of the United States) decision.

The 2022 SCOTUS decision also does not consider women who might want to be defined by a contribution to society other than via motherhood.[9] In effect this decision is collapsing female sexuality, once again, as in the story of Eve, into reproduction. America has now legally regressed 50 years to reinstate government control over—only female—bodies, despite the clear majority of the country's citizens not wanting to see *Roe* repealed.[10] (In the midst of preparing this chapter for publication, SCOTUS turned the clock back 50 years again in the area of improving race relations through its decision to end affirmative action in college admissions. The concomitant SCOTUS decision of ruling that religious beliefs trump equal access and treatment to all US citizens—including LGBTQ individuals—seeking business services, suggest a further regressive turn and movement in today's Supreme Court.)

Going forward, elements of the 14th amendment's clauses of "due process and equal protection" could be legally mobilized on the reproductive justice front in the unalienable respect for liberty that is embodied in basic human differences. The 9th amendment also lends itself to future legal challenges regarding "not enumerated" rights of the constitution belonging "to the people"—and are not to be commanded by the Supreme Court to the states. Lastly, the 13th amendment's speaking to the basic right "not to be bound to servitude" can and should be used to challenge the anti-abortion ruling as binding—and reducing women to being a vessel of reproductive servitude.[11] Ruby Warrington, in her book *Women Without Kids*, has suggested the falling birthrate in America over the past five decades is a statement that more women feel freer to choose a life without motherhood.[12]

## Maternal Power

Among the women who do *choose* motherhood as part of their adult identity, millennial women, perhaps more clearly than earlier generations, are seen reinfusing motherhood with the long-suppressed verve and fierceness of Lilith derived from the very life and death power every mother in fact holds. The brief video postings of the tennis star and business entrepreneur, Serena Williams, coaching her four-year-old daughter on her killer tennis backhand is a simple and endearing example of this verve and fierceness. Modern and even post-modern society's portrayals of motherhood so often do not include this aspect of inherent female power.

Another secret source of maternal power that millennials and Gen X currently hold is that of Lysistrata. In Aristophanes' play, Lysistrata, the title character, led women in persuading men to stop fighting each other and to begin negotiating by encouraging women to tie their sexual availability to their warring men's getting to the negotiating table.

Today there is yet another opportunity. Another kind of Lysistrata card could be played in terms of maternal power. Research is reporting that in the world generally, but especially in the purview of large and powerful countries like the US and China, we are headed for a state of dwindling non-replacement of population.[13] This gives women leverage as never before to *demand* (rather than to lobby for) tax incentives for businesses to re-hire mothers, to incorporate childcare infrastructures, and to develop mentoring programs specifically for returning caretakers of children as *conditions* for motherhood. But adding the ERA as part of our Constitutional architecture would move the needle forward significantly in *all* these areas.

A particularly powerful argument for passage of the ERA is how it would support the economy in mothers' access and return to work by enacting legal requirements for certain child-centered, female- and reproductive-supportive infrastructures. When the pandemic hit America, a huge number of working women just disappeared in a matter of weeks. By spring 2020, 5.1 million mothers of young children had stopped working altogether because parents had to keep children at home during the pandemic. And most often in heterosexual families, male partners were the ones who continued working (oftentimes because men did have higher paying jobs, but not always). This phenomenon hit the generation of millennial women the hardest, of course. And within this pandemic worker landscape, the differential effects across educational and race differences were quite visible. Non-college graduates and non-white women who were less able to work remotely were more grievously impacted.[14]

Women generally suffer more when they stop working because the designation of being a "worker" is often lost to them versus for men in the same circumstances. Most professional women said they were the only parent to consider quitting to take care of kids, and most of them wanted to return to work—but, as is well known for all genders—it is not always easy to overcome the impact of a gap on one's professional resume! *To repeat, passage of the ERA in general would support women's access to work, and, returning to work after childbirth by requiring certain child-centered, female- and reproductive-supportive infrastructures.* Ruth Bader Ginsburg could envision the repercussions of women's rights being only brittlely supported by piecemeal laws, which is why the ERA was uppermost in her mind for the Constitutional amendment's agenda.

The fact that women have yet to be included in the Constitution, even as enslaved men—originally counting only as three-fifths of a person—became "whole" persons with voting rights 50 years before women could vote—bespeaks, and perhaps *shouts* of America's unconscious sexism and misogyny, and could not be more deafening than its silence in the Constitution ...

What marches and protests were for achieving for finally achieving a woman's right to vote (on August 26, 1920) may, in this century, be the power and reach of the internet and social media to bring to group awareness the pernicious effects of unconscious sexism and misogyny. We now move to a consideration of this emerging mechanism of power and influence in the twenty-first century.

## Notes

1 Unfortunately, this effort was afterward plagued by Russian trolls who targeted the Muslim leader, Linda Sarsour, for many months in their attempts to fragment and diminish feminist efforts. By targeting her, the trolls aimed directly for the MAGA base. Overall, according to investigative reporting, the Russians spent over $300 million trolling various places to undermine basic democracy. See Ellen Barry (2022). There was also the critique that the march was "still too white." https://www.nytimes.com/2022/09/18/us/womens-march-russia-trump.html

2 See US House Election Results (2018, November 6). But also interesting, see Rubin (2021) for a detailed description of women's uprising of political resistance after Trump's election and how, in part, it led to the Biden/Harris win in 2020!

3 See the SCOTUS (2022): Dobbs decision, as well as Berg and Woods (2023) for a discussion of the many implications.

4 See Ambrose (November 2022). Of the first twelve US presidents, only two did not actually own slaves. John Adams was one of the two; however, he was quite willing to benefit from slavery in his own household. The effort emerging to track not only which presidents owned slaves, but that of the entirety of Congress, may be a subtle movement toward national reparations.

5 Virginia resident Kati Hornung worked tirelessly toward Virginia's passage of the ERA in 2020, making it the 38th state to ratify. She is now on the campaign trail to get the ERA ratified federally. She has been thwarted by the Republican attorney general (as of the 2022 election), who sabotaged the federal appeal seeking legal recognition of that 38th state being the minimum to amend the constitution.

6 The SDG Index of Gender Equality, looking at gender equality across world nations, only began in 2015, which seems so late in coming but does provide a global measure against which, on several variables, nations can see how they are doing in the movement to full gender equality.

7 Passage of the ERA would improve both access and equality across healthcare. For example, it would guarantee equal coverage of reproductive health, taking into account gender differences, and would give protection against discrimination in healthcare institutions. It would also be a strong factor in promoting, if not requiring, gender equality in medical research and medication trials. Exactly what would be guaranteed in implementation would be hard to specify because federal and state legislation would come into play.

8  For example, in Texas and Mississippi, where abortion laws are extreme, the rate of uninsured children and mothers is very high, poverty is rampant, and social services are weak. For a broad summary of differences between states banning abortion versus not, see Badger et al. (July 28, 2022). Spoiler: states with abortion bans are among the least supportive for mothers and children!

9  See statistics on childless women over the last 50 years in Livingston and Cohn (2010). Also see the Tierce (2021) article: an exquisite articulation of the inner and external experience of having a child when abortion does not seem to be an option and therefore becoming a mother when you are not prepared to become a "good enough" parent.

10  See Pew Research Center (2022) for public opinion survey data on *Roe*'s repeal. An NBC poll looking at race and abortion across time from 2000-2019 showed that 46% of white women are pro-life as opposed to 36% of Black women. Political party affiliation is a good predictor for the two main parties, where you can just reverse the statistics of 20-something percent versus 70-something percent to arrive at pro-life (Republican) versus pro-choice (Democrat) positions. The difference is much closer among independent voters—53% pro-choice to 41% pro-life.

11  Appreciation to the attorneys in a non-fiction book group for the discussion of constitutional challenges to the 2022 SCOTUS anti-abortion ruling.

12  See Warrington (2023).

13  See Cilluffo and Ruiz (2019) for more information on this. The world's declining birth rate is, in part, due to increasing economic development for women (within the caveat that global capitalism has generated more financial inequity), less religiosity, but also, due to the failure of government to make work and parenthood more viable via infrastructure that supports such a family structure.

14  See Bateman and Ross (2022) and Kochhar (2020) for data and impact on the working populations most impacted by the pandemic.

## References

Ambrose, S. E. (2002). Founding fathers and slaveholders. Smithsonian; Smithsonian. com, November. https://www.smithsonianmag.com/history/founding-fathers-and-slaveholders-72262393/

Badger, E., Sanger-Katz, M., Miller, C. C. et al. (2022). States with abortion bans are among least supportive for mothers and children. *The New York Times*, July 28. https://www.nytimes.com/2022/07/28/upshot/abortion-bans-states-social-services.html

Barry, E. (2022). How Russian trolls helped keep the women's march out of lock step. *The New York Times*, September 18. https://www.nytimes.com/2022/09/18/us/womens-march-russia-trump.html

Bateman, N., & Ross, M. (2020). Why has COVID-19 been especially harmful for working women? Brookings.edu, October 14. https://www.brookings.edu/essay/why-has-covid-19-been-especially-harmful-for-working-women/

Berg, J. A., & Woods, N. F. (2023). Overturning *Roe v. Wade*: consequences for mid-life women's health and well-being. *Women's Midlife Health*, 9(1). https://doi.org/10.1186/s40695-022-00085-8

Cilluffo, A., & Ruiz, N. G. (2019). World population growth is expected to nearly stop by 2100. Pew Research Center, June 17. https://www.pewresearch.org/short-reads/2019/06/17/worlds-population-is-projected-to-nearly-stop-growing-by-the-end-of-the-century/

Kochhar, R. (2020). Hispanic women, immigrants, young adults, those with less education hit hardest by COVID-19 job losses. Pew Research Center, June 9. https://www.pewresearch.org/short-reads/2020/06/09/hispanic-women-immigrants-young-adults-those-with-less-education-hit-hardest-by-covid-19-job-losses/

Livingston, G., & Cohn, D. (2010). Childlessness up among all women; down among women with advanced degrees. Pew Research Center's Social & Demographic Trends Project, June 25. https://www.pewresearch.org/social-trends/2010/06/25/childlessness-up-among-all-women-down-among-women-with-advanced-degrees/

Pew Research Center (2022). Public opinion on abortion. Pew Research Center's Religion & Public Life Project; Pew Research Center, May 17. https://www.pewresearch.org/religion/fact-sheet/public-opinion-on-abortion/

Rubin, J. (2021). *Resistance: How Women Saved Democracy From Donald Trump.* Harper Collins.

Supreme Court of the United States (SCOTUS) (2022). *Dobbs v. Jackson Women's Health Organization.* https://www.supremecourt.gov/opinions/21pdf/19-1392_6j37.pdf

Tierce, M. (2021). "The Abortion I Didn't Have." *New York Times Magazine,* December 5.

US House Election Results 2018 (2018). *The New York Times,* November 6. https://www.nytimes.com/interactive/2018/11/06/us/elections/results-house-elections.html

Warrington, R. (2023). *Women Without Kids: The Revolutionary Rise of an Unsung Sisterhood.* Sounds True.

# Chapter 11

# Warrior Work

## Ground Zero 2.0—Digital Worlds

### The Sorcerer's Apprentice

We start this chapter with an animated childhood story that is an apt metaphor for our current internet world—where big creative fantasies also freight insufficiently examined unconscious consequences. The story is Walt Disney's cartoon, The Sorcerers' Apprentice. The scene is the Sorcerer, Mickey Mouse, the Sorcerer's magic wand, the broom, and the water buckets Mickey is tasked with filling.

When the Sorcerer left the room, Mickey grabbed the power of the magic wand to make the broom do his job—that of filling the water buckets—only to discover he did not know how to stop what he had commanded to start. The water was becoming a flood. Finally, in desperation, he tries to stop the broom by chopping it into pieces—only to see the splinters grow into more and more brooms following his initial command. In the end, Mickey must be saved from drowning by the return of the Sorcerer himself. What we do not see, however, and perhaps need to see, is the Sorcerer talking to Mickey about his actions. Neither do we see the Sorcerer questioning himself as to why he left his magic wand lying around so carelessly. In what way might he unconsciously have wanted Mickey to "act out" something he did not allow himself? If he were to ask himself these questions, how much would his Sorcerer's work and his own sense of himself be clarified? And one more question: if the Sorcerer had been a Sorceress and/or Mickey was a Minnie— or Mickey and Minnie were a couple left with the task—would the story proceed and conclude any differently?

Stephen Hawking, the world-renowned physicist, once wrote that artificial intelligence (AI) is the greatest threat to the survival of mankind—much less its flourishing.[1] Maybe or maybe not. It is still important to ask: are we following in the footsteps of Mickey Mouse? Are we, as a group, proliferating machines and technologies that, so far, we have been able to control by touch and voice? But for how long can we control this magic wand? During a 2022 chess match between a young boy and a robot—after one move by the robot, the boy jumped quickly to make his next move, whereupon the robot reached

DOI: 10.4324/9781032677309-13

across the board and broke the boy's finger. Now naturally the robot design-
ers said this was a malfunction![2]

Are we proceeding, too, unconsciously and (with too much masculine
ethos), believing that we can completely control this technology to our
benefit, but having not yet considered that (out of our sight) these machines
could become able to move about the room with their own intentions?

Moore's Law in computer science predicts that our computer power will
double approximately every 18 to 24 months.[3] Surely that timeframe is faster
now? Understandably, there has been an explosion of fascination, and thinking, about what computers can do for us.[4] For example, in medicine, computer
data analysis assists both in training practitioners and assisting in difficult
and complex diagnoses and treatment decisions. Also, very tiny drones can
be directed to survey and move within very small spaces of physical disasters
to search for survivors and provide simple medical assistance. At the opposite
end of the spectrum, however, is the example of how the military has made
use of drones in surveying enemy territory and making precision (or *almost*
precision) strikes. Drone operators were trained in and, indeed, treated the
task as if they were playing a video game. *Almost* precision strikes led to
unintended carnage. And with no anticipation of unexpected consequences,
and no mental health support for drone operators, PTSD and suicides began
to mount among drone operators.[5] One wonders whether if women had
overseen such programs or if more drone operators were women, would the
emotional status and mental health concerns of drone operators have been
apprehended sooner?

After-the-fact-thinking is insufficient thinking when it comes to the widening implications of the human/machine relationship for individual and group
well-being. How will the human/machine interface be woven into our social
fabric? Has there been an "excessive" *lack of broader thinking here*? Are
these technologies to be primarily about conquest, or dollars, or ascendance?
What is in the gap of unconsciousness here? One need only look back a few
generations to see the implications of endpoints *not thought enough about* in
the development of nuclear power—concerning how it was to be developed,
and tended to, in terms of public safety and betterment.[6]

In the arena of America's economy, there is a strong masculine ethos that
allows creators and funders not to factor in implications and endpoints.
Instead, the driving impetus is to thrust forward toward financial success—
until big problems or *outright disasters* command attention. We think about
the profound cultural, and indeed, worldwide contributions of the iPhone—a
computer and communications device in the hands of virtually all of us. And
yet, could we not see, in advance, that young people might become prey to
adult predators, and to one another, via the abuses of such a device? Were
there a balancing presence—perhaps a more feminine presence—in the beginning, combined with an appreciation of the role of the unconscious in overall

human functioning, perhaps the Wild Wild West of the twenty-first-century IT world might have expanded differently, more thoughtfully.

## Misrecognitions

In the following, we bullet-point a few places where our collective minds have denied or mis-recognized the existence of unconscious currents and where the masculine principle has dominated—to the detriment of public well-being.

- "Move fast and break things," Mark Zuckerberg's famous motto of early Facebook days, has not ultimately served the world at large. Starting his trajectory with a site to rate co-eds' attractiveness, Zuckerberg moved initially toward building on the ideals and power inherent in relationships. And yet, the evolution of Facebook "moved fast" into the stream of capitalism—with a vengeance—leaving to the side or "breaking" much of more feminine relational ideals. With total executive power, and no apparent attention to the unconscious currents of American society, Zuckerberg's Facebook has shifted to a different implicit motto: "Company over country." And so, we have now a country within a country run by a single omnipotent leader.[7]
- Twitter, Tesla, and SpaceX are also all companies led by only one man—Elon Musk—who, despite hiccups, ultimately purchased the entirety of Twitter (now known as X). It is his parallel kingdom to Zuckerberg's Facebook, Instagram, and WhatsApp dominance. Musk is now grappling with considerations of freedom of speech, and the material truth of such speech. We must also assess the power of words with or without such foundations, and, in addition, must define the individual responsibility of any tweeter to others. Known as a provocateur and a shoot-from-the-hip Tweeter himself, what can be anticipated? Discontinuities in services and distortions on the platform are expected as thrashings abound, while Musk seeks financial stability. And despite Musk's concerns, or maybe because of them, about the impact of AI, he has launched a small AI company (xAI) of his own, that is expected to link up in some manner with Tesla, to work on complicated scientific and math problems and pursue greater understanding of the universe, especially "dark matter." (A waiting symbol to be socially recognized as a beckoning echo of the unconscious.) This is taking place all the while under the watchful eye of Lina Khan, millennial chair of the Federal Trade Commission, who seems to have a finger on the pulse of what is at stake!
- The delay in response to the proliferation of misinformation on both Facebook and Twitter was substantial in the 2016 election and beyond—monitoring and ramping up intervention only under governmental

pressure. We now operate in an online universe where "alternative facts" are presented without sourcing. This has opened the door to international interference in our elections and a nation divided over which "facts" it attends to as we approach the 2024 presidential election. Under increased governmental surveillance, Facebook is now budgeting $5 billion in self-regulatory efforts in this arena. Compare this, however, with the $10 billion Facebook has budgeted for "Metaverse" development. Metaverse development is the next frontier.[8] Thinking about how to mitigate possible harmful psychological effects may lag far behind creative and financial incentives if the feminine principle is not honored in its development.

- Is the EU—an entity composed of various territories speaking multiple languages—offering the US a challenging model: that of aiming internet policies toward product safety? The US is also composed of many state territories speaking several different political languages. On Twitter/X especially, certain political languages have seemed discriminated against. Will Musk be able to create user and content policies that honor "product safety?" As of 2022, about 30% of Americans get their news from social media, Twitter being a main platform. How Musk will craft a scaffold for discernment of misinformation versus real information is a significant question as the 2024 elections move towards us.[9]
- In the (ever-increasing!) gaming world, Riot Games, whose leadership had been entirely male, was sued in 2017 for sexual harassment and discrimination. Beyond direct compensation in their settlement, the company has pledged to increase their workforce with women and non-binary people by 50% over five years. In 2022, female leadership equaled 20%. This suit and others are helping the gaming world reach to include, however reluctantly, more of a feminine perspective. This feminine principle shows up in such efforts as CEO and millennial, Laila Shabir (of LearnDistrict, an educational media company), launching a summer camp in 2014—Girls Make Games—for girls and non-binary children to learn the basics of game technology development.[10]

Expanding game content beyond the many shape-shifting options that have evolved, games might also include elements that promote considerations of how the unconscious mind influences workings within a game. In a game format where gamers learn about the interplay of conscious and unconscious parts of the mind, a transformation of thinking may be put on their horizon. New things on the horizon are often seen first by the young. For instance, to be able to stop your character's action and choose an option to realize something in the game—if that realization is in a zone of possible truth—moves your character forward in the game somehow differently than the usual paths.

AI has become the race to win in global competition—stirring deep anxieties and foretelling dire consequence if China were to win. But what does *winning* really mean? Recent AI apps such as DALL·E 2, Lensa and ChatGPT—while wonderful to play with—also bring along with them the undertow of issues of personal privacy, data collection, plagiarism, and compensation for artists' and writers' creative productions.[11]

The unconscious mind, besides creating, can also move to disrupt, and indeed, to destroy. Communications theorist Marshall McLuhan's comment, "The medium is the message", calls us to think more deeply—as *we* are substantive to this medium itself.[12] An effort must be made to think with more complexity. And part of that effort is to consciously factor in considerations of both a feminine perspective *and* the role of the human unconscious in influencing human thinking, feeling, and action! It requires time, effort, and many stitches to knit a social net, but not nearly so much time or effort to rip the stitching apart. The feminine principles of care for *all* the members of the human family, across the full scope of their needs and experiences, is too often pushed aside and then devalued and forgotten. Attention to this principle would bring more care and preservation of the stitching of the social netting along the way. It is for this reason we have coined the realm of internet and computer technologies: Ground Zero 2.0 for twenty-first-century feminism.

## Millennials Rising Challenge: Internet Guidelines or Oppressive Rules?

To date, in the online world, there is ongoing disagreement as to how much of an ethical framework is needed to manage and maintain the online world of tech innovations as a free and fair playing field. At the level of global politics and rivalries, elections of those who will set international internet standards are hotly contested—especially between the China/Russian axis and the US and its allies. Closer to home, establishing ethical parameters for US IT companies is currently a major challenge. Yet millennials, especially women, as the current largest generation, are rising to these challenges.

For example, three millennial women have brought forward ethical challenges to the algorithms and aims of AI, with both conviction and the courage to speak out. Millennial Frances Haugen has testified that in the case of Facebook, despite its knowledge that Instagram was having a negative impact on fully one-third of teenage girls, nothing was done. Millennial Timnit Gebru, the former co-lead of the ethical AI team at Google, publicly named the pressing need for funding of independent AI research outside of the profit motives of companies and the universities closely linked to them. DeepMind, now owned by Google, fired Gebru from her position as co-lead of the ethical AI team when she raised certain ethical issues. Millennial woman, Lina Khan, current chair of the FTC, has focused her vision for shared oversight to participate in the ever-expanding frontier of IT and AI. To date, she has already acted to prohibit one Facebook merger as an unfair move toward establishing a tech monopoly and has also filed a lawsuit to prohibit Microsoft from obtaining the gaming company, Activision.[13]

Meanwhile, male feminist millennial, Ben Grosser, associate professor of new media at the University of Illinois, and successful IT innovator, has served as a significant disruptor online. He has pointed out that if Facebook and similar platforms simply stayed with a chronological feed versus focusing entirely on growth, then issues of hate speech, trolling, and manipulating the medium would significantly diminish, if not disappear.[14] Grosser's dissenting, disruptive, and artistic creations all serve to remind the larger societal group that *IT and its platforms are just us.*

During the pandemic, many people worked remotely, and a significant percentage of people want to continue to do so, even as the pandemic has become endemic. It appears that the work world is moving on the shoulders of the millennials toward a "hybrid' model—combining home-working with working in offices. Pre-pandemic, wearable devices tracking employee movement were already available and being used by some companies (e.g., Amazon). Surveillance software, however, is now available, and is being used to track and give feedback to users (and to their supervisors). This is true even concerning workers' *cognitive states*, not just measurable performance data. Will we see more of such tracking with more off-site worker time? When and where can the public assert "freedom to think" away from their employers? And if not now, when? Will there be a protection for the working public that can be counted on?[15]

In this direction, Ben Tarnoff in his (2022) book, *Internet for the People*, argues for de-privatizing the internet and taking it out of the business/profit model through the call for public investment in establishing and ensuring an egalitarian internet.[16] His idea frames a clarion call for ramping up and bringing in the feminine—the feminist sensibility—and a sensitivity to unconscious influences to this "biggest game in the world" so that relational and mental health values will not be extinguished by a thrusting toward purely financial and growth-oriented aims within the IT domain.

Really, the IT world is but a new geography for longstanding group work on gender and racial equality. Both hateful "isms"—sexism and racism—fuel online trolls. On the other hand, there is a reparative field of play here as well … It is not hard to imagine the creativity possible online with simple tag lines such as: "What my unconscious revealed to me today about myself" or "From the gap came …" and similar on TikTok, YouTube, Instagram, Twitch, Snapchat and whatever new platforms human beings can generate from the interplay of conscious and unconscious parts of their mind—to share themselves with and/or challenge society's broad denial of the relevancy of the unconscious to human functioning.

## Finally: An Iconic Image For This/Our Time

We began this chapter proposing Ground Zero 2.0 for twenty-first-century feminist resistance with the Disney cartoon of the Sorcerer's Apprentice. We end now with another iconic image that captures what we believe to be seminal to the feminine, the role of the unconscious, and the future growing world of IT. We're referring to the logo of Apple computer. The hope here is that seeing this Apple logo in the future will never again be the same.[17]

One of most successful businesses in America, and indeed the world, is the computer company Apple. How many years now have we been seeing the Apple logo on computers in movies, television, and streaming videos? The frequency of its appearance has only increased over time. And what do we see beside the laptop itself? We see an apple—recognizable immediately to everyone in the world, almost. But it isn't just any apple. It is an apple with a bite missing. In this moment, Eve of the Bible, and her bite of the apple, may be evoked. So, there is a gap, but there is no small piece sitting beside the apple to give the impression you could fill in that gap. The gap just is. In other words, the gap is integral to the design itself. And in that split second of seeing the apple, from a leading power of the IT world, two things are evoked: a space marking the unconscious being integral to human design, and the still missing feminine elements in our culture. They all come together synergistically. In a flash, the Apple logo is iconic in more ways than just a successful business!

Steve Jobs, again, in his often-intuitive leading way, left a complex message in that iconic Apple symbol for the twenty-first century. We are each a single apple. Each of us has a space/gap inside of us—that dynamic unconscious. We may feel in sync—by birth or cast—with socially understood or prescribed forms of identity—or maybe not (i.e., apple/male, or pear/female, or carrot/X, let's say!). But, whatever the array of possible identities, in this century, IT will become more and more a player in how we each deal externally with the internal space within.

Now perhaps Steve Jobs did not really intend to say any or all of this with his Apple logo with a gap, but Jobs certainly did know that the world of computers and the internet lent itself to a wide array of human uses, and that these possibilities will only exponentially grow across this century. If we are not to suffer a twenty-first century as "Patriarchy 2.0," an awareness of the role of the unconscious in human functioning—and a feminine sensibility—must grow in its presence and participation in digital worlds.

## PS—And One More Thing ...

### Feminism's Work—In the End is to Know That it is Ongoing[18]

In the Netherlands, there lives a reminder about twenty-first-century feminism. The Netherlands is country at the mouth of three rivers, with the

North Sea ever threatening its boundaries. The country lived as a very wet delta until the eleventh/twelfth century, when the first real barriers began to be built to dry the land below sea level and get rid of the excess water through various means in order reclaim land (named *polder*) from the water. Yet, it was not until the twentieth century that a huge effort by the government (taking many years) was made to reclaim over 2000 square miles of land through a system of dams. This was not to be government land, but sold to its citizens. Today some 400,000 people live and own pieces of that land. This is only possible because a system of dams was built, and must be vigilantly maintained lest the sea once again claim ownership.[19]

Instead of resignation to a secondary existence, or claiming equality piece by piece, as the early Dutch did for land, perhaps the twenty-first century offers us the opportunity to realize full *human*, not just gender or racial, equality—all the while knowing whatever framework and boundaries of such established equality is, it must always be tended to, lest some of the darker, rather than the shining seas, of our human unconscious rise and once again swamp the land of conscious intentions for human justice. Such conflicting tension, as with the relationship of sea to land, is elemental to our human condition and requires ongoing work of attention and resistance as needed.

### *A Bit of Humor* …

And, yes, feminists *do* have a sense of humor! Humor with a purpose—so we add an act of play to a bit of wisdom from Shonda Rhimes (producer/writer of *Grey's Anatomy, Scandal, How to Get Away with Murder, Bridgerton, Inventing Anna*) who once said, "Work doesn't work without play." Can you imagine an evocative catchphrase on your T-shirt, scarf, other casual clothing or somewhere else to engage conversation? For example …

All these items of clothing could be conversation-starters! Imagine, for instance, for Figure 11.1, a scarf with: "*21st century Feminism: A Netherlands Project*" on it. People might ask, "What does this mean?" It is an opportunity to play with that metaphor—to explain what it takes to claim psychic territory that is constantly subject to erosion. Imagine, for Figure 11.2, a tank top with "*Lilith—I'm with Her*" that people might ask: "Who is that?" Imagine for Figure 11.3, the T-shirt with "*Mind(n)-ing the Gap*" written on the front and "*In absence is presence*" written on the back, that this T-shirt opens a conversation about how we have things to learn about ourselves beyond our conscious words or intentions—in what may be left out, in the *gap*—there may be something else to tell us. Imagine in Figure 11.4, the T-shirt with "*Unconscious Matters*" written on the front of the shirt and "*In absence is presence*" written on the back, as a way of saying we all have two parts of our mind—and that both play a role in our lives, every day!

Figure 11.1 Scarf: *21st century feminism: A Netherlands Project*
Artist to be credited in acknowledgeements

Figure 11.2 Tank top with *Lilith—I'm with Her*
Artist to be credited in acknowledgeements

Figure 11.3 T-shirt with *Mind(n)-ing the Gap*
Artist to be credited in acknowledgeements

*Figure 11.4* T-shirt with *Unconscious Matters*

Artist to be credited in acknowledgeements

## Notes

1 See Rory Cellan-Jones's (2014) piece where Stephen Hawking warns artificial intelligence could end mankind.
2 See Maishman (2022). Notably, the president of Google has said that AI is huge for Google's future, but in multiple articles in *The Washington Post* there are reports of significant trouble among those working on AI projects—both in terms of the aims of projects, supporting data, and value differences regarding public welfare. People have been fired; people have left voluntarily.
3 Moore refers to Gordon Moore, Intel's co-founder.
4 When an AI-generated painting won an art competition in 2022, it began the conflict about whether it could legitimately be considered an artist's work—not unlike the argument years ago about photography as art form and whether a photograph could be a legitimate submission.
5 See Saini et al. (2021).
6 Early nuclear weapon testing did not even protect the observers, despite knowing of its damaging and lethal effects. Later power plant accidents raised questions as to whether appropriate precautions were even in place and then whether clean-ups afterwards were indeed adequate.
7 See the excellent article on Zuckerberg by LaFrance (2021).
8 Metaverse's virtual reality offerings bring an even greater simulation of presence and touch that, in theory, can bridge distances between people and add to hands-on learning versus book/lecture formats. Metaverse is where Zuckerberg has planted his next flag for the future, while also competing with a faltering Twitter/X by launching the Threads app. Interconnectivity in the Metaverse is increasing, especially among millennials and Gen Z, even as it can bring a parallel subtle experience of alienation when that sense of intimacy in the online playing field does not easily transfer into IRL (in real life).
    Further, a virtual reality dating site, *Nevermet*, was launched on Valentine's Day 2022 with the hope of reducing the emphasis on looks and "swiping left or right" on dating apps, as well as providing a greater sense of contact in multiple

online arenas. And yet, simultaneously in the absence of being face to face, there is also the presence of an even more pernicious experience available to online perpetrators of verbal, physical, and sexual assaults, especially directed toward women players. Interpersonal conduct in VR is still in its earliest phase of dealing with this phenomenon—even as it is still struggling on regular online sites.

9  The "Eliza effect" is a term referring to the tendency among human beings to give, or attribute, humanity to those actions of inanimate things/objects/processes that "feel" human-like. The "Eliza effect" was named by Joseph Weizenbaum, who created the first early therapist chatbot.

   If disinformation was a problem in 2016 elections with just bots, how much more complex and pervasive will the disinformation be with the more sophisticated AI content-generating chatbots of 2023 and beyond? Already conflict exists between those who attribute sentience to these machines (Philip Bosua), actual intelligence in GPT-3 system of OpenAI (Sam Altman, CEO), or only complex forms of computations (Alison Gopnik of UC Berkeley AI research group).

10 Other groups of women promoting and community building efforts include Women who Code, Black Girls Code, and Girl Develop It. Research has reported that the code women write is often rated higher than men's code, but only if gender is not identified.

11 Lensa enables the user to make artistic selfies using uploaded photos of self and using artists' work in databases without artist permission or compensation. ChatGPT produces written responses to posed questions drawn from linguistic databases—worries here include both plagiarizing writers' work and potentially eliminating the jobs done by human beings in a large swath of economic sectors.

12 Marshall McLuhan's (1964) *The Medium is the Message: An Inventory of Effects* introduced the seminal notion that the medium of communication carries its own effects which can be more impactful than the content itself—almost certainly true in the digital world. With television, to just appear on television itself became an end goal—quite separate and supplemental from whatever the televised content might propose. Thus it is in the digital world, where the possibility of "going viral" through ripple re-postings, where many more people see a message/image beyond its first posting, having a magnifying impact, soon became "its own motivation" for anyone posting a remark on social media. This is an additional or supplemental effect of the digital medium to the impact of the posted content.

13 See the Federal Trade Commission's December 8, 2022 official report.

14 See Oremus (2021).

15 See Farahany (2023) for notes on how in China, the government is already tracking employees across various industries. See also, *The New York Times* interactive article (August 14, 2022) about employee tracking and productivity.

16 Tarnoff (2022) points to Americans paying the most for broadband connections, but the US only ranking 14th in its connection speed capability. The material body of the internet is still cables following historical pathways that will require updating and expansion.

17 It is said that Jobs liked the name Apple because it would show up in the phonebook before any competitors! Our suggested iconic image is not to over-idealize Steve Jobs, who was a complicated man. And we won't delve into the potential implications around his repeating his own parental abandonment with his first child. For a balanced look at his life, see Isaacson (2021).

18 Griffith (2020) details the necessity of ongoing co-operative work to establish and tend to the goal of full gender and human equality.

19 Winchester (2021) describes, in fascinating detail, the evolution of land development and ownership in the Netherlands.

## References

Cellan-Jones, R. (2014). Stephen Hawking warns artificial intelligence could end mankind. BBC News, December 2. https://www.bbc.com/news/technology-30290540

Farahany, N. (2023). *The Battle for Your Brain: Defending the Right to Think Freely in the Age of Neurotechnology*. St Martin's Press.

Griffith, E. (2022). *Formidable: American Women and the Fight for Equality: 1920–2020*. Simon & Schuster.

Isaacson, W. (2021). *Steve Jobs: A Biography*. Simon & Schuster.

LaFrance, A. (2021). Facebookland: The social giant isn't just acting like an authoritarian power: It is one. *The Atlantic*, November 17–20.

LaFrance, A. (2021). The largest autocracy on Earth. *The Atlantic*, September 27. https://www.theatlantic.com/magazine/archive/2021/11/facebook-authoritarian-hostile-foreign-power/620168/

McLuhan, M. (1964). *The Medium is the Message: An Inventory of Effects*. Penguin.

Maishman, E. (2022). Chess robot breaks seven-year-old boy's finger during Moscow Open. BBC News, July 24. https://www.bbc.com/news/world-europe-62286017

*New York Times* (2022). August 14, https://www.nytimes.com/interactive/2022/08/14/business/worker-productivity-tracking.html

Oremus, W. (2021). Why Facebook won't let you control your own news feed. *The Washington Post*, November 15. https://www.washingtonpost.com/technology/2021/11/13/facebook-news-feed-algorithm-how-to-turn-it-off/

Saini, R. K., Raju, M. S. V. K., & Chail, A. (2021). Cry in the sky: Psychological impact on drone operators. *Industrial Psychiatry Journal*, 30 (Suppl 1), October. https://doi.org/10.4103/0972-6748.328782

Tarnoff, B. (2022). *Internet for the People: The Fight for Our Digital Future*. Verso.

Winchester, S. (2021). *Land: How the Hunger for Ownership Shaped the Modern World*. HarperCollins.

# Chapter 12

# A Call to Arms

## Re-Sistering

In 1985, Aretha Franklin and Annie Lennox recorded the song, "Sisters are doing it for themselves":

> *Now there was a time*
> *When they used to say*
> *That behind every great man*
> *There had to be a great woman*
> *But in these times of change*
> *You know that it's no longer true*
> *So we're comin' out of the kitchen*
> *'Cause there's somethin' we forgot to say to you, we say*
> *Sisters are doin' it for themselves*
> *Standin' on their own two feet*
> *And ringin' on their own bells, we say*
> *Sisters are doin' it for themselves*[1]

Now, almost 40 years later, this necessity not only remains, but is even more urgent in our changing times. The time of patient waiting—the time of trying to persuade enough heterosexual white men to support full gender equality in all sectors—is so, so long past. The 2022 Dobbs decision at the Supreme Court, once again negating female bodily autonomy and life choices, only underscores this reality!

Early in the 2000s a popular phrase emerged—"The twenty-first century will be the century of the woman" and/or "The future is female." Now, nearly a quarter century in, perhaps it is time to make a turn on this phrase to broaden the base of feminism and increase its force and velocity with respect to achieving full equal human rights. What if, instead, we begin to think of the twenty-first century as being "The century of the feminine."

DOI: 10.4324/9781032677309-14

*Psychically, to occupy a "feminine" stance is essentially to embrace a relational position wherein the human values of social justice and shared responsibility to, and for, others is foundational. In other words, to stand in "the feminine" is to operate in a theater of care parallel to, and on parity with, the precious individual freedom that Americans cling to so tightly.*

Occupying a "feminine" psychic position would not be predicated upon biology per se, although biology certainly carries an effect. Neither does embracing the psychic identification of being a "woman" necessarily guarantee one is carrying a feminine perspective. Nor would claiming one part of identity as a man, or a trans-man, necessarily exclude one from also holding a feminine position.

Were twenty-first century American society to seat itself in a feminine position more explicitly, the adoption of a Biden/Harris legislative agenda would have been easily accomplished in the US Congress. A partial endorsement arrived in the passage of the Inflation Reduction Act and with Biden's college loan forgiveness of up to $20,000. Biden may not be our first woman president, but he may in a way be *exactly* that—in the same sense that Bill Clinton was called the first "black president." Biden is most certainly the first president in the lifetime of most of our readers to be so firmly planted in the soil of the feminine that he offers a counterpoint to America's long-standing commitment to patriarchy.

Moving from the societal/group level to the individual, the question then becomes this: irrespective of biology, what subjective stance and values does a person embrace *psychically*—primarily a feminine one or more primarily a masculine one? What does that person resonate more with: what is good for the whole of the human family or what is good for his/her, individualistic part of the transaction.

Another facet of a "feminine stance" is germane here: that of embracing a fluidity between the feminine and masculine aspects of oneself, and not necessarily insisting on a bifurcated and fixed split. President Biden, for example, appears to hold the masculine and feminine parts of himself as co-equals. He is a man with sisters—(that helps!)—but also, a man who was a single parent—having to both mother and father two young children for five years.

Adopting a more feminine frame of reference individually and societally would open a very wide door to include many people of varying gender expressions, psychic identities, body morphologies, and genetic biologies.[2] It would also inevitably result in loosening gender from its prescribed (and proscribed) ties to heterosexual partner choice.

Twenty-first-century feminism has its work cut out for it! One need only examine the voting patterns of white women in the 2016 and 2020 presidential elections to see that most straight white women supported Trump, the indisputably more sexist candidate. We can hypothesize that this group of white women includes those who have been 100% anti-abortion (which Trump promised by way of appointing anti-abortion justices), as well as women invested in the secondary benefits, protections, and partial absolutions from work/economic expectations that are provided in a patriarchal system.

To be fair, if we look backward, feminism has never entirely stood in the "feminine" in its own outlook or its practices. Historically, it appears that in each successive wave of feminism (as some describe feminism), a group of women have been sidelined or have been actively excluded for fear of alienating men and/or certain white women.[3] In the first wave of feminism of late nineteenth and early twentieth centuries, those sidelined were Black women, who to their credit, refused to be consigned to the sidelines! In the second wave of feminism of the 1960s and 70s, Black women were partially included, but often told to turn their volume down a bit (e.g., the first woman presidential candidate, Shirley Chisholm), while non-heterosexual women were actively excluded. Progress was made toward more inclusion in the third wave of the 1990s to the early 2000s, and fourth waves (2010-ish on), but clearly, we have miles to go![4] Twenty-first-century feminism's aim is to be truer to its feminine values, inclusive of the voices of feminists of all stripes and colors and biologies. The color of change in twenty-first century feminism *must* truly be polychromatic and gender inclusive. And, at the same time ...

## Feminism and Race

In 2020 America, the murder rate rose by 30%.[5] No doubt the stress of the pandemic seeded an evacuation of rage and despair into more violence, but—as is always the case in this country—violent rage and despair landed differentially by race and gender. Among females in 2020, five Black women and girls were killed *every day*—the homicide rate for Black women being three times that of white women.[6] In the transgender population, according to an ABC report, 73% of tracked homicides between 2017 and 2021 were of Black trans women, though they make up only an estimated 13% of the transgender population. Also, according to data from the Centers for Disease Control and Prevention, homicides in the US increased by 20.6% from 2017 to 2020. At the intersectional nodes of race and gender, such data mirrors how much Black women as a group absorb and reflect America's violence toward women. Worldwide, women and girls in 2021 were murdered over 50% of the time by family members—primarily by men. (Of men murdered, only about 11% were killed by someone they knew.) UN worldwide official statistics report that violence against women has remained stable over the last ten years.[7] *Intersecting* across all categories of male violence toward women over these ten years, before, and beyond, there remains *a systemic disavowed unconscious* bias against women that fuels the conscious, psychological, and ordinary day-to-day unfulfilled desires and expectations of men that can then result in retaliatory violence toward women of all colors.

## Feminism and Gender

An ongoing feminist challenge of this century is to discern who is considered a "real sister" in the long struggle for equal rights for all gendered human beings, and what social expectations are in fact humanly reasonable, rather than gendered assigned. The axis of gender conflicts seems ultimately to proffer the question of "who and what is a real woman?" and "who and what is a real man?" And by what authority or power does society accord to either identification certain roles, rights, and privileges?

A truly feminine stance would have the intention of separating gender identification from biology or sexual orientation. This is a current politically hot, divisive, and confusing issue in America, that appears to have trained its focus on the trans-gendered community and the non-binary discourse.

Despite considerable societal expectations, and even demands for gender conformity, the "trans-ness" of gender has been increasingly and irrepressibly evident in America. Since Christine Jorgensen underwent gender reassignment surgery in 1952, there has been an increasing tide of awareness that multiple gender positions/identities are possible and indeed necessary to fit the experience of many individuals.[8] The word "trans-gender" began to appear in books in 1976, but since 1980 it has spiked upward.[9] The sheer number of words referring to multiple gender positions/identities has proliferated during the past 20 years in the attempt to recognize individual human specificity in the realm of gender.[10] State and federal legislative actions have been reaching for a containing frame around this fraught and shifting territory during the first 20 years of this century. These legislative efforts often reflect political affiliations. For example, the Republican legislative law HB-2 of North Carolina restricted bathroom use to sex-assignment at birth—with no means for its actual enforcement (and guaranteeing more people urinary tract infections!). HB-2, under pressure by an American Civil Liberties Union (ACLU) lawsuit, was rescinded when money issues and losing sports-hosting venues became too costly! Gender followed the money in this case—not human rights.

The roots of the trans issue are deep and wide in the human psyche, stirring primitive anxieties regarding what is stable ground for the basic questions of "Who am I? And who are you?"

So, what are the divergent positions on gender in twenty-first-century America?

- One position is that sex is assigned at birth, based on genital parts. It is deemed to be a fixed identity grounded in biological sexual difference. All state anti-trans laws commonly hold this perspective.[11] (This, however, does leave out those with hormonal disorders in utero and at birth. Ovotesticular disorder of sex development (ovotesticular DSD), for instance, is a rare disorder in which an infant is born with the internal reproductive organs (gonads) of both sexes (female ovaries and male testes).[12] So much for sex assignment at birth!
- Another position is that *psychic* identification eclipses physical characteristics. Therefore, how one feels psychically in terms of occupying feminine or masculine energies will be more primary to identification as a woman or a man than physical sexual characteristics. (Altering body parts may or may not be a part of securing this gender identification intra-psychically.[13]) This gender identification position is one that supports non-traditional families, wherein the emphasis is on the importance of having a "psychological parent" versus a biological parent for providing the necessary foundational feminine principle in the early years of life (see Chapter 4). The rapidly-evolving reproductive technologies also indirectly underline this position, where egg production, fertilization, and external gestation of human embryos become ever more loosely tied to biological gender.[14] Within a few decades, reproductive technology may enable egg production from stem cells from any gender (even a single individual) and completed gestation-to-birth in external wombs.[15] Thus, in the twenty-first century, we may aspire to become "the century of the feminine," where society moves further to emphasize the psychic function of a feminine principle operating within primary caretaking parents.
- Yet another position is that gender identification is mobile, and thus, should not have to be stuck in either binary position, as a woman or a man, but instead, ought to be recognized in its fluidity and complexity. In this position, both biological and psychic identifications are in interplay. This would be one way to understand individuals who say they are non-binary. This perspective reflects some of the reasoning behind shifting from singular reference pronouns of "she" or "he" to "they," "them," and "theirs." In 2019, the Merriam-Webster dictionary added a new meaning to the word "they." The word "they" can now also mean "a single person whose gender identity is non-binary." As awkward as this may seem, sound, or be, in everyday conversation, it is important to remember that such awkwardness also

accompanied "Ms." when it was introduced into the lexicon in the 1970s—and now it is not given a second thought. Perhaps another third word will emerge, but in any case, history tells us that language can change things.

Common to behavior in groups, a general split has formed in America focused on freedom of expression versus fear. Some see the entire uprising of the trans phenomenon as yet another attack on a basic pillar of stable (some would say fixed) gender definitions undergirding personal identity, family, and societal order. Akin to arguments against gay marriage rights, this aggressive stance is rooted in fear—fear that could abate over time along similar lines, as gay marriage did, if America's polarization begins to lessen.[16] The gay marriage discourse shifted over time from the social focus of "deviant sexuality" to the "right to love." In its wake, social resistance softened and morphed quickly into marriage acceptance, thus leading to the 2015 Supreme Court ruling. Such a turn in the winds of disquietude regarding the trans issue could occur when there is more lived experience— actually "seeing" that there can be more than one stable way to be, or to do, gender. And yet, the voiced threat by Supreme Court Justice Thomas after the 2022 Dobbs anti-abortion decision, to "re-visit decisions of gay marriage and sexual orientation" is a dark cloud forming once again. Of the 390 legislative anti-trans bills introduced in various states in the last four years, only 39 have passed.[17] And at the same time, a 2022 Gallup poll shows the continuing march of gender diversity in the fact that 21% of Gen Z cite a LGBTQ identification versus 10% of millennials; 4% of Gen X; and 3% of boomers claiming the same!

Since the 1970s, significant ambivalence and conflict about trans-gender identities has been percolating.[18] There is more than one split among feminists themselves on these issues. One sub-group claims trans-women as another ally in the ongoing struggle for gender equality—period.[19] Another sub-group feels that at least some trans-women reinforce gender stereotypes through extensive surgical interventions. Surgical interventions are thought by some to undermine "the feminist cause" so to speak, by over-emphasizing traditional femaleness in terms of dress, presenting "woman as masquerade" and as the "object of male desire."[20] Another more confrontational sub-group mounts resistance to embracing trans-women identities at all because they do not stretch to see anything beyond the meme that trans-women are really men undercover—invading and co-opting a woman's space.[21] And, as for trans-men—these individuals can be accused of abandoning the feminist cause altogether—or "changing teams" by putting a masculine identification first.[22] Thus, conflict and feminist confusion abound here—and yet, this is human thinking in action.

## Trans-Formations and a Place of In-Between-Ness

There is, however, another (perhaps more feminine) vantage point from which to view the range of trans and non-binary phenomena. It is not a new idea, but an idea whose time may be arriving, on the coattails of another idea.[23] "Trans-ness" itself can be framed as an emotionally intense discourse grappling with the very concept of in-betweenness, or thirdness, or "binary-plus" thinking. This may be an evolving concept situated in gender conflict right now—but it is not entirely limited to that context. Author Ruby Warrington is suggesting the term "a-reproductive" in order for child-free or childless people to move beyond binary categories. If there has been anything that has been increasingly destructive across the last few decades during the fundamentalist Right's rise, it has been the jettisoning of, and attack on, critical thinking—where two opposing positions may be in conflictual discourse while also holding the possibility of generating a third idea or position. Living in an era of increasing polarization/splitting for decades now—right versus wrong, good versus bad, real woman versus not, real man versus not, and on and on—has only led to a malignant polarization and destructiveness. In this way, the trans discourse is pregnant with its possibilities.

One of the ultimate beneficial outcomes of the entire trans tumult would be to help bring the culture closer to recognizing the value of giving up on the idea of black-and-white thinking, or "fixed certainties." Instead, imagine a culture in which human effort is to embrace and occupy a position of tolerating uncertainty—such that within any specific discourse, there might be a space where something new can be created in-between. "Non-binary" may be a twenty-first century opening term for this point of view. So, perhaps there might be space to move toward a broader concept of thinking—in "binary-plus" terms. There will always be a certain tension between what an individual may need to embrace—whether about gender or other identity features—to feel authentic in their individual self-expression and what society may consider currently acceptable and normative.

## So, Moving Onward

To re-frame the twenty-first century as the "century of the feminine" is to offer a simpler, but wider frame—a frame where a feminine principle is truly and fully brought into the workings of the social orders of politics, education, business, and technology. This frame would proffer a long-missing balance to centuries of masculine/patriarchal hegemony—without being stuck in a biological rendering of gender.

To parse the word "resister" into "re-sister," then, is to highlight a dual agenda: (1) the resistance to anything less than full gender equality, which may happen in part through expanding feminism itself by re-sistering the movement; and, (2) the recognizing and accepting twenty-first century feminism as a "Netherlands project."

As noted in Chapter 10, the Netherlands, with great sustained effort, carved out and claimed a more viable land mass from the sea. To accomplish this, the government had to build a working infrastructure to dry out the underwater land, and then to create an infrastructure to guard against regressive undertows of the sea seeking to reclaim its loss. Unconscious sexism reaching toward conscious misogyny is a wide and deep sea that may always persist to varying degrees within the human species. Feminism must work continuously on the infrastructure level—not only to gain land on which to walk equally among men—but also, to keep and shore-up social infrastructures to stand against the regressive pull of the unconscious sea of sexism.

So, in the end, the twenty-first century "call to arms" for more "warrior work" requires two kinds of arms. Arms are needed to fight conscious as well as unconscious sexism and misogyny by ratifying the Equal Rights Amendment (ERA) and moving with alacrity into the world of digital technologies. Yet, a different kind of arms are needed to gather and hold together more sisters in continuing to pursue both full gender and racial equality—twin aims that in the twenty-first century cannot truly be separated. When the Franklin/Lennox twentieth-century song said, "Sisters are doing for themselves"—all kinds of sisters standing in the feminine principle will be needed.

Looking forward then, perhaps additional new mythic foundations for the twenty-first century would be useful to inspire further action. The resurrection of the creation story of Lilith has offered an archetypal woman whose repressed energies are returning. Thus, in our next chapter, one such mythic foundation is offered—in the KVM chronicles.

## Notes

1   From the song "Sisters Are Doing It for Themselves" by Lennox & Stewart (1985).
2   See Monro et al. (2021). Individuals who are born intersex have, in recent years, been advocating that any surgical interventions at birth or in early infancy, which would place a person in one gender or the other, be postponed until the individual can decide for themselves to choose a binary or non-binary position .
3   See Schuler (2021): excellent and engaging.
4   See again Elisabeth Griffith's (2022) comprehensive review of American feminism—the good and not so good.
5   See Gramlich (2021). In 2022, homicides actually fell 4%.
6   See Beckett & Clayton (2022).
7   This according to the United Nations Office on Drugs and Crime (UNODC) (2022) worldwide research on violence toward women and girls—reporting five were killed every hour by a family member.
8   See Boomer (n.d.) and Doctor (2007) for biographies.
9   Google's Ngram on trans-gender has tracked the emergence of trans-gender across time. Trans-ness was a complicated and conflictual issue in the 1970s within feminism then too, but not so much on the public stage as has been the

case since the turn of the century. It has become a rallying cry by the Republicans to overturn protective trans civil rights laws and curtail health care. One of the most egregious is the Texas law to prosecute parents of trans kids seeking medical treatment.

10  See Morgan et al. (2020). The Federal Committee on Statistical Methodology shows the proliferation of terms and identities. Gender as a term linked with sex roles opened with John Money's clinic for intersex and transexual individuals—established in 1960s but still tied to biological roots versus analysis of ascribed social descriptors, which came later.

11  See Clark (2022) for numerous examples.

12  Fausto-Sterling (2000) provides a comprehensive overview of the genetics of sex determination—spoiler, it's not a binary. John Money's contributions to the discourse around sex and gender in the latter half of the twentieth century cannot be overstated either. See Bullough (2003) for information on Money's life and work.

13  See Teich (2012).

14  See Witt's (2023) excellent article on the rapid rate of reproductive research.

15  Again, see Witt (2023).

16  There are only two US states that do not have at some level of government LGBTQ representation. In 2022, LGBTQ candidates ran in all 50 states—two lesbians became governors (Massachusetts and Oregon).

17  According to Branigin & Kirkpatrick (2022), noting bills affecting trans athletes' sports participation, gender affirming health care, and ID restrictions to biological gender at birth are primary targets. In 2022, 174 anti-trans bills in 36 states were introduced: 26 became law in 13 states according to the Trans Legislation Tracker (2023). These bills are aimed at excluding trans-females from competing in women's sports—prohibiting medical professionals from treating gender identity issues—i.e., hormone blockers or supplemental hormones or surgical interventions to align psychic gender identification with anatomy at birth; making official identification cards (i.e,. driver license or state ID cards) align with the gender assigned on original birth certificate. The national Republican party, along with many Republican majority state legislatures, are making trans and non-binary identities a major fear-based issue to mobilize their voters. The number of state anti-trans bills introduced 2023 into 2024 will most certainly increase.

18  See Schuller's (2021) chapter on TERF (trans-exclusionary radical feminist) gatekeeping and the trans feminist horizon for an excellent history of transgender over the decades.

19  Trans women are feminists—see Stone (1991) on the argument for biological bodies as open to social inscriptions—a companion text of sorts to Judith Butler's (1990) *Gender Trouble* (Routledge).

20  Trans women as undermining the feminist cause by endorsing stereotypical female presentations.

21  Janice Raymond (1979) was the first to argue that trans women were, in actuality, men co-opting the feminist position for their own gains and is the founding text of the TERF position—an essentialist stance.
    For this wing of feminism that opposes transgender identities—emphasizing the biological grounding of gender and female difference, we offer the provocative image of the space and water ship of Chapter 13 as a jumping off point for further artistic expressions celebrating biological femaleness. This spacecraft image of a potential "real thing" is literally drawn from the actual organ of a female clitoris. Aware that for some this craft form may be seen as provocative, we offer instead that it is only so because the penile, phallic inspired forms of maleness have, to date, dominated western societies.

22 Trans men as abandoning feminism—ain't necessarily so.
23 See again Kyla Schuller (2021) on the decades' earlier idea of trans-identities as a "thirdness."

## References

Beckett, L. & Clayton, A. (2022) "An unspoken epidemic": Homocide rates increase for Black women rivals that of Black men. *The Guardian*, June 25. www.theguardian.com/world/2022/jun/25/homicide-violence-against-black-women-us

Boomer, L. (n.d.). *Life Story: Christine Jorgensen*. Women & the American Story. https://wams.nyhistory.org/growth-and-turmoil/cold-war-beginnings/christine-jorgensen/

Branigin, A., & Kirkpatrick, N. (2022). Anti-trans laws are on the rise. Here's a look at where—and what kind. *The Washington Post*, October 14. https://www.washingtonpost.com/lifestyle/2022/10/14/anti-trans-bills/

Bullough, V. L. (2003). The contributions of John Money: A personal view. *The Journal of Sex Research*, 40(3), 230–236. http://www.jstor.org/stable/3813317

Butler, J. (1990). *Gender Trouble: Feminism and the Subversion of Identity*. Routledge.

Clark, J. (2022). Sex assigned at birth. *Columbia Law Review*, 122(7), November. https://columbialawreview.org/content/sex-assigned-at-birth/

Doctor, R.F. (2007). *Becoming a Woman: A Biography of Christine Jorgensen*. Routledge.

Fausto-Sterling, A. (2000). *Sexing the Body: Gender Politics and the Construction of Sexuality*. Basic Books.

Gramlich, J. (2021). What we know about the increase in US murders in 2020. Pew Research Center, October 27. https://www.pewresearch.org/short-reads/2021/10/27/what-we-know-about-the-increase-in-u-s-murders-in-2020/

Griffith, E. (2022) *Formidable: American Women and the Fight for Equality: 1920–2020*. Simon & Schuster.

Lennox, A. & Stewart, D. (1985). "Sisters Are Doing It for Themselves". On *Be Yourself Tonight*. Words & Music by Annie Lennox & David Stewart. Copyright © 1985 by Universal Music Publishing International MGB Ltd. All Rights Administered by Universal Music — MGB Songs. International Copyright Secured. All Rights Reserved. *Reprinted by Permission of Hal Leonard LLC.*

Monro, S., Carpenter, M., Crocetti, D. et al. (2021). Intersex: Cultural and social perspectives. *Culture, Health & Sexuality*, 23(4), 431–440. https://doi.org/10.1080/13691058.2021.1899529

Morgan, R., Dragon, C., Daus, G. et al. (2020). *Updates on Terminology of Sexual Orientation and Gender Identity Survey Measures FCSM-20-03*. https://nces.ed.gov/FCSM/pdf/FCSM_SOGI_Terminology_FY20_Report_FINAL.pdf

Petrosky E., Blair J. M., Betz C. J. et al. (2017). Racial and ethnic differences in homicides of adult women and the role of intimate partner violence—United States, 2003-2014. *MMWR Morbidity and Mortality Weekly Report* 2017; 66: 741–746. DOI: http://dx.doi.org/10.15585/mmwr.mm6628a1

Raymond, J. (1979) *The Transexual Empire: The Making of the She-Male*. Beacon Press.

Schuller, K. (2021) *The Trouble with White Women: A Counterhistory of Feminism*. Bold Type Books.

Stone, S. (1991). *The Empire Strikes Back: A PostTransexual Manifesto*. Duke University Press. DOI: https://doi.org/10.1215/02705346-10-2_29-150

Teich, N. M. (2012). *Transgender 101: A Simple Guide to a Complex Issue*. Columbia University Press.

Trans Legislation Tracker (2023). 2023 anti-trans bills: trans legislation tracker. Translegislation.com. https://translegislation.com/

United Nations Office on Drugs and Crime (UNODC) (2022). *Gender-Related Killings of Women and Girls (femicide/feminicide)*. https://www.unwomen.org/sites/default/files/2022-11/Gender-related-killings-of-women-and-girls-improving-data-to-improve-responses-to-femicide-feminicide-en.pdf

Witt, E. (2023). The future of fertility. *The New Yorker*, April 17 https://www.newyorker.com/magazine/2023/04/24/the-future-of-fertility

# Chapter 13

# A Myth for Now and Going Forward

## The KVM Chronicles

The challenges of our twenty-first century summon inspirational myths to help reach full gender and racial equality. Author Maria Tatar has suggested, but not detailed, in her book, *The Heroine Has 1001 Faces*, that the arc of a feminine hero is simply not parallel to the masculine hero.[1] So, framing Lilith as that invisible "Other Woman"—how might those repressed and/or split-off feminine energies continue to return in mythic form? What obstacles await? What, if any, weapons, and strategies would be needed to nudge human equality to its next steps? How might a feminine heroic arc look? Would there actually be more than one pathway of feminine heroism?

Forty-five years ago, boomers launched the "Star Wars" mythological series. Today, Gen X, and millennials especially, have invested deeply in the development of the Marvel universe and its symbolic challenges. Certainly, myths are not our sciences any more, but they do endure in carrying psychic wisdom in search of social expression and integration. The evolution of Darth Vader in Star Wars teaches how goodness can turn destructive when the best of intentions reaches for, and is consumed by, a fantasy of omniscience: I know better; and omnipotence: I will make it so. (Sound like any political figure you know?) The Marvel multiverse is revealing to all—that with superpowers comes great responsibility, as well as this truth: there is no escape from one's own personal experience of doubt, fear, and vulnerability.

Surely there is more that mythmaking could bring and teach us? A new myth of feminine heroism may help provide American society with something artists call the "middle distance." In the visual field of painting, something seen at a "middle distance" helps to frame the overall perspective within a painting. When the middle distance "something" is not there, the painting's perspective appears distorted. For example, Georgia O'Keefe's painting "Faraway, Nearby" shows an animal skull in the near distance and a mountain range in the very far background. Without having something painted in the "middle distance" area—or in between—the near ground figure of a cow skull seems overly big, too much present, as it were, almost scary, while the background landscape of mountains appears too small and just too far, far away.[2]

DOI: 10.4324/9781032677309-15

Are we now living in a time where certain phenomena are too near, too big, too scary—e.g., male mass shootings, increasing gun suicides, ongoing police killing of unarmed Black citizens, the return of government control over women's bodies—such that the horizon of true gender and racial equality seems indeed far, far away? Even with the visible and vibrant presence of a female vice president, Kamala Harris, the end distance of full human equality still looks so far away. New myths for these times with needed "middle distance," that is to say, a place where unconscious elements and currents are regularly included as human factors to be considered, perhaps then, full human equality might not appear so, so far away.

## The KVM Chronicles: A Myth for Our Time

Many millennia have passed since Lilith left Adam and the Garden of Eden. Adamantly refusing to submit to less than equality in all things, she spoke God's name, flew away, and created her own world on a cluster of verdant islands. And perhaps because of the power of her speaking the name of the Supreme Being, she was able to make a veil of invisibility between the mainland and the nestled islands. This veil served as protection to her world-in-the-making, but simultaneously made her characteristic strengths fall under a veil of unconscious repression in the world she left, leaving her replacement as first woman, Eve, with less.

There were certain human beings who could see across the veil into her world and at times would try to cross over—some with good intentions and some not. With time, provisions were made for both types of cross-over people—the good ones and the bad ones.

When individuals of dark intent were not repelled and were able to cross over, they were captured and sequestered within a reconciliation area. And, although sequestered, these individuals were free to move within that space where two different kinds of mirrors existed—strategically placed in many places—and these locations changed daily. One kind of mirror reflected dark and disturbed thoughts in images that spoke specifically to the individual's fears underneath their aggressive thoughts. Another kind of mirror caught the more positive or hopeful thoughts and reflected enhanced and elaborated positive images of who they could become and what they could do. And, always, there were specialized, trained guardians available to talk to at the end of each day about the personal images that these individuals had encountered in their mirrored selves that day.

After a while (and this could be a long while, or not so long), psychic transformation occurred where self-awareness about the why and how of their own darkness increased alongside an accumulating set of positive self-identifications. The person sequestered needn't be so anymore. It was known that most previously dark intruders elected to stay and start a new life on this side of the veil, but some wanted to return home—even though they knew that once they crossed the veil again, all memory of their time in the Islands of Lilith would be lost—but not the internal structural changes they had made.

Over many centuries, a great multitude of creations and kinds of children were born of Lilith among these Islands—some virgin births emerged from the union of differences within herself and were held by the sea. Others were born from loving, generative relationships with others. Surreptitious visits across the veil to the mainland over the centuries had kept Lilith abreast of how other human beings lived, developed, and changed in the various parts of the world—but nothing she ever saw in the world of gender or race relations made her want to return to that mainland world of Adam, only to resume one version or another of a second-class personhood.

And for another thing, she remained irked by the Bible creation story of Eve that followed her leave-taking. The woman who had been put in her place of origin was literally a white-washing of female identity—both in skin color and in overall diminishment, having been made from the borrowed rib of Adam. So, only due to an early twenty-first century dream did her senses and mind became especially alert and alarmed about the world she had left behind. Lilith had used a spoken word to fly off from Adam to freedom, but in her dream, she heard simply one spoken word repeated over and over—Mayday, Mayday, Mayday!

Somewhere, coming from the northwestern hemisphere, a dream call was coming for her return: an urgent call for revolutionary help to bring gender and human equality—finally—across that finish line. Knowing such dreams can portend big changes, and make big demands, Lilith decided to make multiple visits by sky to see a place now called United States—supposedly the most powerful world nation. What she saw was that it was not so united and in fact appeared to be in a self-destructive spiral.

On these multiple visits, she saw great wealth disparity producing excruciating pain; she felt wide swaths of hate and aggression among people who did not share the same thoughts and feelings. She saw many, many people using drugs to escape and cope with their painful lives, leading to their death. She saw many more black and brown people incarcerated. She saw, too, more and more guns, followed by more and more impulsive gun violence—mass shootings affecting many children, as well as adults. Lilith trembled with their fear, suffering, and despair.

All that Lilith witnessed disturbed her greatly. She felt acutely the suffering from whence the dream call came—a building siren. Even her sky visits themselves became a disturbance because some pilots managed to see her aircraft. And since it was like nothing they had ever encountered before, public discussion of her sightings was taboo for years (since UFOs were only seen as threats to humanity's survival), when in fact it was clear that human beings were their own worst enemy. In 2022, for the first time, the US government acknowledged these sightings and lack of knowledge about them. (In retrospect, however, people of the future would come to realize that these sightings were in fact a heralding of big changes that were to come.)

Lilith interpreted her dream of Mayday, Mayday, Mayday as a "call to arms" that she could not refuse. Yet she also realized it was a call that required much more than her energy—much more than one, feisty, mouthy, sexy, powerful old woman, however revolutionary she might be. Among her many children, Lilith thought immediately of one set of triplets as a team she could perhaps send and who surely would be up to the job; children birthed from a union, yet born of the sea, providing them with some extra advantages in seeing, and in changing their physical forms.

This threesome had been especially nurtured by frequent visits from their space/time parent who had a strong investment in them, and as a result, they had all developed a wanderlust themselves. Also, each one had specialized abilities. So, when Lilith thought about it, they were in fact made for this challenging "Mayday." They could be the team to respond to the Mayday "call to arms." As triplets, she had named each of them with a rhythm of three syllables: Kaitani, Vidrio, and Meluma; but when she was scolding them or calling them from afar, each child went by a single beat nickname—Kai, Vi, and Mel.

They really were an impressive trio. They all shared the traits of being a hybrid of water and land beings, most evidently in the additional transparent eyelid, that when consciously closed, could allow them to see something, as if through water, of the unconscious aspects present in the speech of any person standing before them. Because of this ability, Lilith had to teach them about how, and how not, to understand this feature of themselves, and when and how to use it—as well as emphasizing its use for good rather than for manipulating others for their own selfish ends! Since there were three of them together, they had had lots and lots of practice before they ever joined the world on their own! Also, as part of their hybrid sea and land nature, each had a chameleon ability to alter skin color, gender, and sexuality, bringing them a lot of freedom to play within—but also—a lot of responsibility.

Despite their shared characteristics, each one in their separateness also had unique abilities. Naturally, or un-naturally, each also had vulnerabilities and darker elements within to contend with. So it was that all these qualities and forces for the good—both individually and collectively—of course, paired with the darkness in each one, and as a group, would have to be thought about if they accepted this challenge to cross the veil. Put all together, Lilith thought, they could become a magnified positive force for equality and justice.

**Kai:** The oldest of the threesome by eight minutes—something she never let them forget—was fiercely protective, physically the strongest, and the most athletic in the water and out. Early on, she wanted to be a member of the Guardians tending to the veil shielding their territory from the rest of the world. She was a true Warrior. Kai's greatest vulnerability was having a bit of a temper and being too quick to see the wrong, the bad, and the threat, and to magnify it. This could make for impulsive protective aggression on her part!

**Vi:** The ultimate visionary planner of the three. As the middle one, she was often trying to figure out the best way for them all to play and work together. She was always thinking and strategizing wherever she might be and about whatever. She especially loved solving problems in systems—so she would be a great asset in bringing needed structural/organizational changes in multiple arenas, i.e., government policy, internet technologies, big business and world finance. She was truly a comprehensive Strategist. She could be controlling at times—though her heart was good—thinking her strategy or plan was obviously the best! Thinking and planning so much, she could also be naïve in the emotional/feeling realm and vulnerable to manipulation.

**Mel:** the youngest of the three, but only by eight minutes, but was still the baby after all. She was the artist creator of the three—the most playful, creative, and sensual—which at times could go a little out of bounds! Not everything could be about playing, her siblings said, but Mel did not see why that had to be so! This willingness to experiment and explore could leave her blind and vulnerable to the aggressions of others. Her playfulness also meant that her concentration and focus could waiver, making her less than reliable and vulnerable to distraction—but she was certainly the true Artist!

Lilith thought preparatory work would be needed to send them off to this final revolution, assuming they were willing?! But then, of course they were!

Kai said, with fierceness, "We were made for this challenge." She set herself the task to design a craft for three that could be powered in air and under water—knowing Lilith's visits by air had been noticed. She focused her design on weapons that would disarm, disable, and immobilize rather than destroy.

Vi said, "We will need to develop strategies in a number of arenas in multiple places." She began thinking immediately about the interface of discriminatory governmental/business policies and structures sequestered by gender and race and what products or services could be introduced by non-male people of many colors that would have a big impact and make for a big jump forward!

Mel said, "How many individual shapes can we take and use in this project? How much artistic freedom and play would be possible?" She knew that "this project" would require her focus, persistence over time, and her faith in the mission. She also knew of herself that she was vulnerable to losing those aspects when her attention was caught by an attractive, creative other!

All three decided that they would take only seven days to prepare since the message had been delivered with such urgency—"Mayday, Mayday, Mayday!" Each day they would work alone but meet at the end of the day and go over their work at supper.

Kaitani would build a vehicle that could fly, sail, and submerge, since Lilith's craft had been sighted and they might need to evade trackers. Vidrio would work out designated cities to live in, how to fund themselves, and how to enter in selected fields that were most in need of the feminine energy-infusion. Meluma would design and create necessary items:

(1) A ring each would wear that could be used to call the others as needed.

(2) A cloak that could serve female, male, or gender fluid forms, cut and woven from that special material that made their islands invisible to the rest of the world. With such a cape, each could disappear as needed. Meluma, who, most often of the three, enjoyed the play of moving between female and male forms, also was aware that the conditions in the rest of world that created the call of Mayday would mean there would be enemies and not simply allies to mobilize—thus a cape was essential.

(3) Mel would also creatively fashion small, compact-sized mirrors from the bigger mirrors of the reconciliation center to be used by them all to seek understanding of the unconscious fears in the psyches of dark enemies and what positive elements were there too: but eclipsed, and yet to be realized. (All three siblings knew that occasionally certain individuals of evil intent were able to pierce the veil of invisibility of their island and so guardians at the boundaries had always been necessary.) And of course, these compact mirrors could also reveal things to themselves as well— they need only to look in the mirror!!

(4) Finally, a double-sided locket necklace—also with a smaller mirror inside that could be opened to catch a glimpse of an unconscious aspect of a person. Beautiful and inviting touch and examination, others seeking a sister's intimacy might move to open the locket—and in doing so, a quick reflection beyond the person's surface might be glimpsed by the sister.

Thus, it was, that all three siblings came to be united in seeing that their aim was in essence to "ferry" gender and racial equality to its end destination. In playfulness, they began to think of themselves as ferry-folks—and ferry-makers—helping selected others to ferry many others across conflictual cultural waters to a shore not yet seen of full gender and racial equality. In their shared sense of humor, they also all knew the sound of "ferry" conjured the word "fairy," and how a woman could be and had, in fact, been diminished by being tagged with this word through time. And, how this same sounding word has been used to degrade men as well. They also liked the paradox of what "ferry-maker" held in its sound—of evoking the world of magic that many young allies might feel inspired to move toward. Each sister, carrying their unique abilities, would search out allies—and kindle within these allies the light of seeing through their eyes how full equality and justice exist as the necessary condition for humanity to continue to survive and thrive. As such, an intensity of focus in purpose would empower them.

With all this in mind, KVM, as the threesome came to be known, began their week of work to launch the project of their lifetimes!

### Third Night Supper

By the third night of their seven days of preparation, Kai, with Mel's help, had a working design for their vehicle—one that could move quickly, and maneuver through both air and water. In contrast to the many vehicles

*Figure 13.1* Craft that fly both in the air and under water

Artist to be credited in acknowledgements

*Figure 13.2* Center of a Ring of Power

Artist to be credited in acknowledgements

inspired on the male phallic form, Kai purposely drew her design from the clitoral form of the female. The three began imagining what additional features might be needed in their ship. The ship's name was yet to be decided

Vi, also with the help of Mel, drew a design for their shared rings' centerpieces, composed of magical colored gems from their islands. A pattern for making the cape of protection was also drawn up by Vi and Mel, leaving color or patterns to be decided individually. In both cases, their designs were subject to revision and consensus before moving on to the making of them. Supper that night was lively and, at times, heated, with discussion swirling in their individual differences in strengths, opinions/ideas, vulnerabilities, and desires all being engaged!

## The KVM Chronicles: Their Journey and Arrivals

The triplets reviewed their schema: Vi called these "Scaffold elements for one feminine arc of heroism"

- Receiving "a call"
- Consulting others and gathering a team
- Discerning needed resources and developing a strategic plan (thinking/emotional strategies for journey and ultimate engagement)
- Dispersing the team with collaborative assignments
- Encountering identified enemies and looking for and enlisting allies/helpers to dissipate resistance versus destroying them
- Implementing strategic plans
- Team assimilating and (versus masculine hero's triumphant return and standing apart) moving toward a social re-organization.

They were ready. But they knew that, without their devotion and ingenuity, and their ardent collaboration, the un-united states would continue to devolve. They knew the time had come.

Consider in these times what you have just read as a prequel to a "call to arms" chronicle in which three uniquely endowed triplets responded—their real stories only beginning when the siblings were leaving their islands. To where, to what, and how would these stories unfold? Well, these stories are for others to imagine, write and illustrate.

## In Summary

In the end, perhaps the striking difference between a masculine heroic journey and a feminine heroic journey could simply be described in pronouns. While the masculine hero often must get help from others in completing the mission, the story remains, and is described as the quest of an "I", as in I, the hero of this tale ... In contrast, the feminine heroine arc may begin as a "we" and end as a "we"—regardless of how that "we" may evolve during their journey and tasks. In the endgame, any gendered (or not) person could take up either pathway of a heroic journey, because heroism need not be adhesively stuck to biological sexual difference.

## Notes

1   See Tatar (2021).
2   Much appreciation to psychoanalyst and author Kerry Malawista (2013) for this notion of "middle distance" coming from O'Keefe's painting,

## References

Malawista, K. (2013). *The Therapist in Mourning*. Chapter 1: "From the far away nearby: Perspectives on integration of loss" (Adelman, A., ed.). Columbia University Press.

Tatar, M. (2021). *The Heroine with 1001 Faces*. Liveright Publishing Corporation.

# Chapter 14

# In the End—A Beginning

The long, thin park of Hains Point in Washington, DC reaches out into the Potomac River. At its end point is a huge sculpture, rupturing the surface of the earth.[1] The sculpture is titled *Awakening*. At first the sculpture is more present in its absence because, walking toward the sculpture, you see almost nothing, and then, you see protruding parts—a knee and a bit of a leg here, a hand and forearm there, a partial head breaking through elsewhere, a foot poking through even further away.

This awakening spirit took shape in Angela Merkel's 2009 remarks to the US Congress, where she gathered energy from the best of the twentieth century, to cast forward "hope" for a greater sense of community across cultural difference in a still unfolding century.

> *"I am convinced that, just as we found the strength in the twentieth century to tear down a wall made of barbed wire and concrete, today, we have the strength to overcome the walls of the twenty-first century, walls in our minds, walls of short-sighted self-interest, walls between the present and the future."*

## For the Now and Moving Forward

In our own post-2016 election processing of the Clinton loss and the Trump victory, three strands emerged over time: the influence of both individual and group unconscious, the phenomenon of excess, and the redemptive power of the feminine. All three emerged and, over time, began to form a braid. Also, there began to arise a wondering alongside this braiding: could these strands offer anything beyond our own mourning process? Could they seed a different way of thinking about "American exceptionalism" and our ongoing pursuit of a "more perfect union"?

Researchers tell us that *for any "new idea"* to really *"sink in"* and become internalized and enacted, *"at least seven exposures"* are needed.[2] Multiple exposures over time, in different content areas, and different formats,

DOI: 10.4324/9781032677309-16

promote the internalization of new information. This is especially true of complex ideas.

In the previous chapters, we proffered multiple exposures to the three strands of this braiding: the unconscious, America's fascination with excess, and the power of the feminine. In Chapter 1, we named our nation's reluctance to appoint a female to the office of the presidency, preferring, instead, a man utterly ignorant of the practical scope and moral weight of a US executive. In Chapter 2, we presented a pictorial image of the unconscious. In Chapters 3 and 5, we explored the geode of excess, how this has gripped our culture, but how it also may provide access to our own potential national future. In Chapter 4, we looked at the importance of the feminine, and what happens in a political and social culture when its importance is diminished. Chapter 6 presented our ripeness for cultural change—America at a tipping point. Chapter 7 took us back to the feminine, and into the mythical world of Lilith as a model and champion of the feminine. Chapter 8 looked historically at the two most powerful generations in our lifetimes, and at the sweeping changes in the world of females: one generation built upon the shoulders of the one before. We continued in Chapter 9 to focus in on two boomer women who have provided international leadership and influence in the context of the cultural power of the feminine. In Chapter 10, we named as "Ground Zero" the active pursuit of the Equal Rights Amendment, which would reverse the unimaginably immense unconscious gender gap in our founding document, the US Constitution. Similarly, in Chapter 11, we named the unconscious gender gaps in other places, especially in the ever-expanding tech and internet fields. On the playful side, in Chapter 12, we considered the interplay of feminism, race, and gender. We proposed a new arc of heroism—a female heroine, Lilith, with associated mythic stories that highlight the interplay of gender fluidity, creativity, and unconscious processes—as yet another way of working with, and illustrating, this weaving. We even featured clothing as a possible medium of expression of these ideas. In the end, we were aware that every manner of exposure facilitates a group first to entertain, and then to internalize new ideas. In Chapter 13, then, we presented a new myth—the KLM Chronicles—featuring characters who embody all that we've touched on in our previous thinking and writing.

### For the Many Moving Forward—Some Final Thoughts ...

Psychoanalyst Christopher Bollas coined the expression "unthought known" to denote a territory deep within our unconscious mind.[3] What he meant by this is that there are things we know deep within ourselves, that influence how we think, how we feel, and how we behave, but we don't know that we know them and we don't know how much they are guiding (or misguiding) us. These "unthought knowns"—these unconscious messages—in fact, exert an energy within us, a push to be unveiled and known. We can invite and be open to such messages, or we can close ourselves off from them. But, without an effort to make a sort of third space of openness for encountering our "unthought knowns," we remain "unconscious," but also subject to the influence of these unthought knowns. Our unconscious prompts us in a vast panoply of ways—in our attitudes and our decisions, in whom we love and how we treat them, in impulsive words or actions, in behavioral excesses. These are all examples of directional indicators that can invite us to that "third space of openness"—a place to be curious about, and possibly (in that space), to encounter our own "unthought knowns." These are messages which we might use—as individuals and, collectively, as a nation—to determine truer and better pathways for our time on this Earth.

Of course, it is never possible to empty any person, group or nation of either negative or positive unconscious elements. It is simply and profoundly a foundational human condition that our mind and self are divided between conscious and unconscious elements. But we can know more about each part of our minds. One person or one nation can choose to relate to, and work with, the conscious and unconscious parts of the mind—or *not*—but we cannot escape their effects. One way of opening ourselves as a culture to our "social unconscious" might be to become more deliberately conscious of how our "isms"—sexism, racism, misogyny, etc.—are expressed in language. This might entail bringing attention to and naming such unconscious elements as the everyday speech which freights such "isms." This could, in turn, bring the social unconscious more into play, making it more real, more accessible, and ultimately, more mutable. While heightening our accountability for whatever manifestation of an unconscious "ism" is occurring or has occurred, it could also harness the creative power of language to effect positive change.

Were we, as human beings, to accept on a cultural level the notion that one ideal of humanity is to strive to operate within a "third" thoughtful space, a social transformation would indeed occur. It would move society collectively to "stand more in the feminine" and its associated relational structures and values. Simultaneously, it would lessen the desperate, grasping impulse to defend and retain the kind of hyper-individualism which is deeply rooted in the American white male patriarchal order. Finally, a recognition of and embracing of movement between the conscious and unconscious parts of mind would eventually become integrated into the definition of what it means "to be human." Such an integration would shift the basic categories of what is "required" or "expected" to fulfill the meaning of "human being-ness."

### Understanding a Human Rhythm: Steps Forward And Back

As the circle of light increases, so does the circumference of darkness around it.[4] There is always more to see, more to understand. A final question suggests itself as we close: what, collectively, has America been experiencing in its movement from Obama to Trump to Biden? Several steps forward seem to have been followed by giant steps backward. One way of understanding such a development is taken from our experience as clinicians. In a psychodynamic psychotherapy, when a person's internal world is beginning to make shifts to positively reorganize itself, the old ways of defending oneself against past real, or current imagined, threats often begin to re-emerge. It's as though the old ways of being are beginning to lose a dominant position of control within the person's psychic organization, and the childhood parts of the self arise in protest: "Wait a minute here! Let me show you how much you still need us to be in charge." There is often a temporary resurgence of self-defeating, but formerly self-protective, attitudes and behaviors.

*Change* that modifies a person's character *is a process* that involves a steps-forward-and steps-backward rhythm—*over time*. The interplay of conscious and unconscious parts of mind takes time to reorganize. This is true of individuals, but of the collective as well. Any fantasy of Obama as our first post-racial president was just that—a fantasy—but it also represented many steps forward. For example, not only was he our first Black president, but also Obama's healthcare initiative, his promoting of climate care, his appointing of a world ambassador for women's issues, his initiating the DREAM Act—were all policies standing more on the feminine principal side. (This Act, proposed in 2001 but not ratified, granted temporary conditional residency to illegal immigrants who were brought to the US as minors, giving them the right to work, and, with further qualifications, the possibility of permanent residency.)

Trump's election as a pinnacle of excess and patriarchy has represented steps backward. But then we saw steps forward again in America's voter turnout for the 2020 election, where more citizens voted than in the past 120 years—especially the young—who voted for Biden/Harris. This was a step forward in favor of human equality. And yet, as if exhibiting another gasp of the intransigent, bullying patriarchy, 147 of US House Republicans voted against the Electoral College's certification of the Biden/Harris win. A steep rise in state voter suppression laws followed, and multiple efforts to reconfigure state political positions were aimed to undo the will of the voters in the 2020 election, also making for unfair elections going forward. The wondering now is: will the 2024 election results return America to another national step forward—as a heralding away from "Trumpism's" excesses—or further steps backward as a harbinger of greater darkness and democracy in decline?

## In Closing—A Beginning

### The 2022 Mid-Term Elections—Plus

Historians describe that when there is a revolution in the recording and transmission of information, the conditions are ripe for *human transformation*.

For example, the Reformation was linked to the invention of the printing press and opening the pathways of knowledge beyond the elite of religious institutions. In the context of the world-changing impact of the internet, humanity is again living in a period where conditions are ripe for a transformation in thinking.

As we were writing this last chapter, the 2022 mid-term elections took place, and the results appeared as a signal that the majority of the country is moving in the "we" direction again.[5] If the decades-long succession of excesses in America has been a signal light to America to wake up to the idea of its own collective unconscious, then perhaps "excess" can indeed provide "access" to messages of unconscious knowledge. And if we indeed are becoming able to access that message, then the 2022 mid-term election results are indeed encouraging. *We propose that the 2022 mid-term election results, rendered by two-thirds of American voters, can reasonably be framed as America's first collective interpretations of its years of excess epitomized in Trump himself, and then, cloned into the excesses of "Trumpism's" adherents.*

Political analyst, Mathew Dowd, described the generally unexpected 2022 mid-term results as a "moment of clarity" in the nation. (Only Michael Moore seemed able to truly "read the room" when he said there will be no "red wave.") Dowd noted there have been other "moments of clarity" in American history. He cited the Civil War and racial equality with the passage of the 13th amendment. He also named a "moment of clarity" concerning gender equality in the passage of 20th amendment, granting women the right to vote. In each case, however, "the moment of national/group clarity" has been followed by 100 years of working it through—with that work of psychic integration continuing. So, a person, or a country, can have an epiphany—a deep and complex insight—but the realization of that insight will require working it through over time.

One partial summary of America's collective 2022 interpretations of Trump and Trumpism's excesses is that two-thirds of the country answered this way to the one-third base:

- *No,* to the infantile omnipotent wishes and claims of omniscience. Everyone but Peter Pan must grow up.
- *No,* to big lies and to bogus words not grounded in material truth—because words do need to matter for any kind of democracy (and civilized society) to exist.
- *Yes,* to basic human fairness—more than one person's needs and desires must matter.
- *Yes,* to one person-one vote being foundational and to all votes counting in American democracy.
- *No,* to the excess of Trump-appointed Supreme Court judges' repudiation of *the right of one person-one body integrity* needed to ensure the reproductive justice that must undergird true human equality.

These interpretations are not explicit in the 2022 election results, yet the idea of putting the conscious mind into a working relationship to the unconscious mind—and the idea that there is a necessity for both feminine and masculine principles to be represented across the spectrum of society and its government—can be read implicitly in these results.

As we close this chapter, other hopeful *heralding signs* and interpretations of the ex-president's excesses can be seen in the indictments reached in the Mar-a-Lago stolen documents case; indictments coming, but not yet detailed, in the January 6 insurrection case; and indictments looming from the state of Georgia regarding multiple attempts to void and/or defraud valid election results. The imaginary omnipotence of the One should not stand in our democracy of the Many—each of whom is entitled to his/her/their say. (By the fall 2023 US elections, all looming indictments against Trump had arrived, and there was continued voter pushback seen in election results within both "red" (Republican) and "blue" (Democratic) states, against the Supreme Court's 2021 anti-abortion (and anti-body integrity and autonomy) Dobbs decision.)

Today, we are only a quarter of a way into this century. In another three-quarters of a century, a transformation in human thinking is possible—in fact a *revolution* in human consciousness. Change that modifies an individual's or a nation's character ultimately must consider and reconcile itself to the fact that human beings always live within, and act out of, a bi-cameral mind. So, can we move from the long Age of pure Reason, to one of an Age of Discernment? Is it possible that twenty-first century feminism could lead us into a new age of perspective, where the naming and establishing of a "working relationship" between the linear, reasoning, conscious mind and the more fluid, unconscious mind, would be deemed necessary—essential even—to achieve gender, racial, and fuller human equality, to preserve it, and facilitate humanity's thriving?[6]

Is America amid just such an emergence—beginning to re-member its parts bit by bit from a parade of excesses—excesses culminating in the personification of excess—Donald Trump—and the subsequent metastases of "Trumpism"? Have we seen accumulating signals of America's collective unconscious pushing for a certain social recognition and response? Has our parade of excesses really been leading us toward an awakening, or has it just been a series of harbingers of darker things approaching—a continuing disavowal of the collective unconscious combined with a turning toward more primitive states of mind within the psychic body politic and within the public itself? If Donald Trump has revealed only one thing to America, it would be the searing consequences that eventuate when the entwined influences of the feminine principle and the unconscious aspects of the mind are blocked—factored out—and remain culturally unacknowledged in our socio-political thinking and policies.

*"It is the very nature of this fight for civil rights and justice and equality that whatever gains we make, they will not be permanent. So, we must be vigilant. Understanding that, do not despair. Do not be overwhelmed. Do not throw up our hands when it is time to roll up our sleeves and fight for who we are."*

Kamala Harris (2016 presidential election night)

## Notes

1   The sculpture was installed in 1980 and author Mardy Ireland encountered it soon thereafter on a run. Some years later, it was relocated elsewhere in DC.
2   See Cohn (2013) His article emphasizes the marketing principle that it takes seven touches (exposures) in different forms to internalize and act on new information. Also, see the classic article from Miller (1956).
3   See Bollas (1987) for more detail on the concept.
4   Paraphrasing of Albert Einstein (1936) "As our circle of knowledge expands, so does the circumference of darkness surrounding it."
5   See sociologist Putnam with Garret (2022) looking across a whole century and suggesting a positive cultural parallel may be at work. There was a shift from the selfishness of an "I" emphasis at the end of the eighteenth century, toward an increasing investment in the "we" in the early nineteenth century, that built over time until it began to fade again in the later twentieth century. May we again be moving from a period of "excess," with its "I" emphasis at the end of the twentieth century, toward a more "we" state of mind now, and in the next three-quarters of the twenty-first century?
6   This would be in parallel to when, in the centuries before the Renaissance, artists were only able to portray objects in two-dimensional space with hints toward that third dimension; but then, artists moved to becoming able to represent an entire scene in three-dimensional space. In the Renaissance, a new dimension heralded a new perspective to come.

## References

Bollas, C. (1987). *Shadow of the Object: Psychoanalysis of the Unthought Known*. Columbia University Press.
Cohn, M. (2013). Seven touches: A basic marketing principle in action. *Social Media Today*, November 27. www.socialmediatoday.com/content/seven-touches-basic-marketing-principle-action
Einstein, A. (1936). Physics and reality. *Journal of the Franklin Institute*, 221(3), 349–382. https://doi.org/10.1016/s0016-0032(36)91047-5
Miller, G. (1956). The magical number seven, plus or minus two: Some limits on our capacity for processing information. *Psychological Review*, 63(2), 81–97. https://doi.org/10.1037/h0043158
Putnam, R. D. & Garrett, S. R. (2022). *Upswing: How America Came Together a Century Ago and How We Can Do It Again*. Simon & Schuster.

# Index

For Product Safety Concerns and Information please contact our EU
representative GPSR@taylorandfrancis.com Taylor & Francis Verlag GmbH,
Kaufingerstraße 24, 80331 München, Germany

Printed and bound by CPI Group (UK) Ltd, Croydon, CR0 4YY
08/06/2025
01897000-0016